D1117721

With Unshakeable Persistence
. . . .

With

. . . .

Unshakeable

. . . .

Persistence

. . . .

Rural Teachers *of*
the Depression Era

. . . .

Elizabeth McLachlan

. . . .

NEWEST PRESS
EDMONTON

Canadian Cataloguing in Publication Data

McLachlan, Elizabeth, 1957–
    With unshakeable persistence : rural teachers of the depression era

ISBN 1-896300-11-1

    1. Teachers—Alberta—History—20th century. 2. Teachers—Saskatchewan—History—20th entury. 3. Education, Rural—

Alberta—History—20th century. 4. Education, Rural—Saskatchewan—History—20th century. !. Title.
LA2321.M34 1999   371.1'0092'2712   C99-900972-9

Cover and interior design: Brenda Burgess
Editor for the Press: Satya Das

NeWest Press acknowledges the support of the Canada Council for the Arts for our publishing program. We also acknowledge the financial support of the Government of Canada through the Book Publishing Industry Development Program (BPIDP) for our publishing activities.

  Canadian Patrimoine
Heritage canadien   Canadä

Cover photographs have been reproduced with the kind permission of:
Joanne Abrahamson (school) and the Burgess family (group photo).

An earlier version of "Murray's Story (I)" was published under the title "Teaching in the Middle of Nowhere," in the May/June 1995 edition of *The ATA Magazine*. An earlier version of "Murray's Story (II)" was published under the tile "Gem of A Year," in the August 22, 1996 edition of *Western People*.

Every effort has been made to obtain permission for quoted material and photographs. If there is an omission or error the author and publisher would be grateful to be so informed.

Printed and bound in Canada

NeWest Publishers Limited
Suite 201, 8540-109 Street
Edmonton, Alberta T6G 1E6

Dedicated to all those who so

generously shared their stories for posterity.

. . . .

Table of Contents

. . . .

Acknowledgements

. . . .

When I reflect upon whom to thank, names come tumbling toward me, avalanche-style. First one—then another—then a shower—then a deluge. Too many people, too little space to properly express my gratitude. Let me at least scratch the surface.

My thanks to writer Barbara Smith of Edmonton, without whose enthusiasm, guidance and encouragement this book would not be. To Diane Reil of Tofield, for always saying "when," never saying "if." To Shari Maertens-Poole of Pincher Creek, for casting an editor's eye over early efforts. To Shirley Roessler, (the mysterious voice on the phone, never heard from before or since), for convincing me at my lowest moment not to abandon the project. (Are you an angel?) To my teenage daughter, Brandi, for rescuing me at the eleventh hour by volunteering to type the manuscript onto disk, when her computer-dumb Mom discovered that's how the publishing industry works these days. To Robert Kroetsch for his keenness, and for his kindness in giving the word, (in more ways than one)! To my editor, Satya Das, and the staff at NeWest Press, Liz Grieve, Kathleen Chiles, and Jennifer Bellward, for walking me through, bearing me up, setting me straight, and calming me down.

To the many, many friends and supporters whose stories, books, phone calls, and letters flowed constantly from across the country. Special remembrance to Murray Robison, Margaret Hill, Dorothea Laing, Annie Tym, and Mary Cooke, contributors who passed away before they could see their stories in print.

Last but never, never least, profound thanks to Dale, my husband, whose unfailing faith in me has made me who I am today. Words will never be enough.

A Thank You Prologue

· · · · · · · ·

This brief prologue is a thank you to the teachers who taught in rural areas of Alberta and Saskatchewan during the Great Depression. This thank you is written by one of their many grateful students.

Those teachers worked heroically, under what now seem impossible conditions, to give us learning skills and knowledge—and an abiding sense of hope. By their commitment they not only kept alive the tradition of learning but also they shaped, in major ways, the rich prairie culture we delight in today.

The individual stories, comic at times, tragic at times, that Elizabeth McLachlan brings together under the title *With Unshakeable Persistence*, become in themselves a series of lessons. They tell us about a past that is already receding from view in the pale light of computer screens. They show us that heroism is not simply the fantasy of television and movie producers; it is often the stuff of daily life. And, most importantly perhaps, these individual stories show us that life in its rural origins is profoundly communal.

I entered grade one in 1933, in a two-room school in the hamlet of Heisler, Alberta. HEISLER SCHOOL DIST.

NO. 3710 1920 was painted in bold letters over the front door of the wooden building.

I went to school by horse and buggy that fall. I was too young to drive on my own, so an older cousin who was also a student came and lived with us. She drove and looked after both me and the school horse, called Old May. I don't know if May was ever young, she was always Old May. In any case, she got me through the next eleven years of, literally, going to school—four and a half miles there (seven km), four and a half miles back.

To get to school we drove three miles (five km) north, to the correction line road, then turned at what was called Philip Hauck's corner and drove east a mile and a half (2.5 km) to the school. On cold days in fall or winter, getting to that corner was a victory; it meant we turned east and the numbing northwest wind that we had been facing was suddenly at our backs. But I won't elaborate. This book is rich in examples that make my experience look like the cushy life.

I will mention, though, the mouthfuls of horsy-tasting hair one received twice a day when, in spring, Old May was shedding her winter coat. I should also add that once I began to do the driving myself, with my sisters Pat and Sheila as passengers, it turned out that I was not exactly a skilled horseman. In the wintertime we drove in what was called a closed-in cutter; a cutter with a small cab on top of it, a small stove inside, and very small windows front and back. I wrecked the whole out-fit three times: once by just barely bumping another closed-in cutter during a three-cutter race.

Each morning when we got to the school yard we unhooked Old May and put her in her stall in the barn.

Then we took our lunch pails, scribblers, and pencil boxes and went up the hill to the school cloakroom.

At that point we fell under Miss Boyle's watchful eye. She was already at work by that time. She taught four grades in one room, and had to be organized right down to the minute. And Miss Boyle managed to combine organization, discipline, and generous warmth in her small and youthful frame, under a head of red hair that instilled awe in her thirty-odd students. (She is, to this day, Miss Boyle to me; I never once heard her first name spoken. Our respect for teachers was nothing short of immense.)

While my parents lived on a large farm in a mixed farming area, becoming teachers seemed to run in the family. One of my favourite cousins, at the age of nineteen, became the teacher in the neighbouring Wanda School, a solitary one-room building set out on bald prairie with a pair of outhouses to keep it company. My Uncle Norbert Weller taught in a series of rural schools, including the Roundhead Creek School, which boasted the first teacherage in the area. And of course a few of my cousins married schoolteachers. Marriages such as those enriched the cultural life and the elaborate kinship patterns of rural communities on the prairies.

The Heisler school grew to three rooms and three teachers. The depression years gave way to the War years. I went away to Red Deer High to take grade twelve the same year that the first school bus rolled down the gravel road in front of our farm. Old May and I were the end of the horse age. In the fall of 1944 I found myself for the first time in a school that had a library room, a science lab that wasn't simply a cabinet at the back of the school room, a gymnasium, running water.

Part of the heroism of those many teachers in rural schools was their teaching with very few resources. And that included—it seems a marvel now—having almost no books. By the time I entered grade four I had read the entire library in our school room. That was not exactly a great feat, since that entire library was located on a table at the back of the room. In any case, because I had read all the books once, and most of them twice, I was permitted to go to the next room to read. As a result, I quite by chance read a novel by Joseph Conrad and another by Henry James. I discovered, to my bewilderment and delight, books that contained mysteries and possibilities that I hadn't ever imagined. And then, talking to Miss Boyle, and to Miss McDonald in the second room, I discovered that they could tell me of still other books, other ideas. They pointed out magical places on a big school map that advertised chocolate bars.

When Mr. Merta replaced one of our teachers who got married and moved away, he decided that school needed a band. In one year he taught twelve students to find some semblance of music in a collection of unwieldy second-hand banged-up musical instruments. That meant we could go to sports days in Spring Lake, in Daysland, in Forestburg, in Hastings Coulee, even as far away as Strome and Bawlf, to perform between baseball games. And that meant that some nights we could stay for the first hour of the dance that followed after the ball tournament and the foot races and a surfeit of Big Orange and hotdogs.

Those rural teachers, generously and seriously and with unshakeable persistence—and that too became a lesson—helped us shape our lives. They taught us with chalk and blackboards and talk in the classroom; they taught us with music and athletic events; they taught us by example.

Those unsung heroes, so eloquently remembered here in Elizabeth McLachan's book, deserve the thanks of all of us. Many of those heroes, after too long a silence, find here in this book a chance to speak their own histories.

Readers, old and young, rural and urban—I invite you to join me in thanking those teachers. Many of us learned to read, to write, to do arithmetic, to memorize and debate, to perform in Christmas concerts, to play scrub during a fifteen-minute recess, to work and laugh with each other—by being their students. All of us can celebrate their contributions to the enduring prairie story by taking this opportunity to learn from their words, from their lives.

Robert Kroetsch

. . . .

Murray's Story (I)

IN 1934, JUST weeks before his twentieth birthday, Murray Robison allowed himself the extravagance of bus fare from his hometown Medicine Hat to Irvine, Alberta. Then he trekked four miles (6.5 km) across virgin prairie to apply in person for his first teaching position. His strategy was to overshoot the stampede of unemployed teachers responding by mail to the single job advertisement. It worked. Perched in the middle of nowhere on the barren landscape, the Schlatt School was a grey, weather-beaten shell. It boasted one room, eight students in five grades, shifting walls, and a leaking roof. Eight months of teaching would net Murray $544. It was a plum job. In the midst of the depression, many of his fellow Normal School graduates fell far short of such luck.

Thus began an experience typical to many rural teachers of the 1930s. While their jobs were to impart knowledge to young minds, their challenge far surpassed that. The rural teacher was woodchopper, water hauler, keeper of the fire, carpenter, exterminator, boarder, translator, and long distance hiker. Many were city-born. Most, like Murray, were barely beyond youth. Challenge indeed!

There was no teacherage at Schlatt. Instead, Murray

was expected to help the depression-worn farmers of the district pay their taxes by boarding with each of them during his term. These farm families were generous and welcoming, but many were German immigrants and the English language baffled them. Murray found German just as bewildering. At once this posed a double dilemma. The elderly couple he boarded with first spoke no English, and neither did the grandson they were raising. Not only was Murray unable to communicate with them at home, but his ability to teach the boy, just entering first grade, was severely limited. "My Normal training hadn't given me much help in trying to teach non-English speakers to speak English," he recalls. School regulations complicated matters further by stipulating that only English be spoken on school property. Murray objected to this rule and frequently ignored it, despite the substantial risk to his job.

During the depression people were at the mercy of whatever means they had to live by. Murray's first landlords were desperately poor chicken farmers. Their only food was chicken, eggs, and bread. Day after day the farm wife put a cold, soft-boiled egg in Murray's school lunch. Before long he came to detest it. Not wanting to appear ungrateful in front of the children, however, he took to disappearing over the coulee hill each noon and secretly stuffing the loathsome thing down the nearest gopher hole.

Another family Murray boarded with raised pigs; salt pork was the mainstay of their diet. Fresh fruits and vegetables were almost nonexistent, and although the local population seemed quite immune to these deficiencies, Murray's less hardy constitution was not. He eventually succumbed to scurvy. Horrified by the diagnosis, the treatment distressed him even more. How could he possibly consume copious quantities of fresh grapefruit before the deprived and longing eyes of his hosts? Sadly and with guilt, Murray kept the precious fruit in his desk, eating it in the late afternoon solitude of the empty schoolhouse.

Meals weren't always a difficult affair. German women were famous for their culinary talents, making meals at times cause for joyous anticipation. Murray recalls one household with particular pleasure: "The interesting thing here was that each day of the week had its own special menu, so every Monday you knew exactly what you would get, every Tuesday likewise, and so on. I loved all the meals but I think Monday was my favourite—chicken stew, dumplings, and apple strudel."

Accomplishing the day-to-day tasks of living was an achievement. In rural environments gas, electricity, and indoor plumbing were unheard of. Perishable food was stored in root cellars or hung down wells. In summer, flies were so thick that everything to do with food, even the drinking pail and dipper, had to be covered. Winters brought relentless cold. Wood and coal stoves provided heat, but only in the common rooms of the house. Frequently Murray woke with the bedclothes frozen to his mouth and an icicle hanging from his nose, a glassy pool of frozen water waiting in the bedside washbasin. On such cold mornings having to share a bed wasn't so bad. Although in general Murray was given his own room, accommodations were cramped. One family had no choice but to put him in a tiny room with their ten-year-old son: one of his students!

Conditions were no better at the school. Each morning Murray stopped at the nearest farm for a bucket of water, which he carried a quarter mile (.5 km) to the school. In

winter he arrived well in advance to start a fire in the pot-
bellied stove. The children began classes huddled in a semicircle around it. Gradually the ink in their inkwells, frozen
overnight, thawed along with their numbed fingers, and
they fanned out into their proper places. One morning a
banana, left overnight and frozen solid, made a perfect
hammer for picture hanging.

Even in mild weather the school was uncomfortable.
The famous southern Alberta winds battered it mercilessly.
"In a really bad wind the whole building would lean lee-
ward," Murray recalls. "If I happened to be writing on the
blackboard, the chalk would skid about two inches [five
cm] with each gust." The building creaked in the wind and
leaked in the rain; dust sifted endlessly between cracks
and beneath sills.

One of the worst problems Murray faced was mice. The
insidious rodents made themselves scarce during the day
but wreaked havoc at night. They got into desk drawers
where they shed droppings and shredded paper. Murray
tried desperately to stem the plague with mousetraps but
the nightly visits continued. One evening while working
late, he heard a soft thump, and then another, come from
the direction of the stove. The mice were dropping down
the air intake pipe and scurrying off on their nightly mis-
sions. "I concluded they must have a nest in that pipe,"
says Murray. "Before leaving school that evening I placed a
pail of water under the intake. Sure enough in the morning, when I arrived at school, there were literally dozens of
big and small mice drowned in that bucket." Murray never
had mouse problems again.

Despite the discomforts, the children enjoyed school,
preferring it to home, where chores always waited. Never

was this clearer to Murray than the Monday he slept in, missing his ride from Medicine Hat where he had spent the weekend. The first train to Irvine didn't leave until noon. From there Murray strode twelve miles (nineteen km) across the prairie to school. He arrived midafternoon and was astounded to find all the children present. Rather than return home when they discovered him missing, they had remained, and the oldest girl, a grade eight student, was standing in as teacher. Fortunately for Murray, none of the students exposed his tardiness, and the school inspector remained none the wiser.

The children weren't always angels. A good number of shenanigans occurred behind Murray's back. It worked both ways, however. His surreptitious trips over the coulee hill to dispose of the odious eggs were also used to have a quick smoke. Other smoke breaks took place in the outhouse, where Murray could count on a few minutes of privacy to enjoy his vice. In such a place it was easy to discard the evidence before emerging with a justifiably satisfied look. Fifty years later, while chatting with a former student, Murray learned the rest of the story. The older boys, fully aware of what he did in the outhouse, took the first opportunity after his appearance to descend upon it themselves, fish out his butts, and smoke them to extinction.

Despite the occasional departure from regulations, Murray always received good reports when the inspector came around. He couldn't be granted a permanent teaching certificate, however, until he taught more students in more grades. With this in mind, in 1936 he moved to the Abelein School near Pashley. "My circumstances were somewhat better at Abelein. I was getting more money, nine hundred dollars, the school was a ten month rather than an eight month school, and I didn't have to board around to help pay the farmers' taxes." In addition, an older student was hired to haul water and tend to the pot-bellied stove. Murray felt positively pampered!

He roomed at Cage Green, the picturesque farm home of the school board's secretary-treasurer. Situated on the banks of the Ross Creek, Cage Green was four miles (6.5 km) from the school. Each morning Murray crossed the creek on foot, hiked one and a half miles (2.5 km) along the valley floor, half a mile (one km) up the coulee hill and two miles (three km) across the prairie to school.

His custom of walking wasn't unusual. Foot power was rivalled only by horsepower for transportation in rural areas during the depression. Even those who had cars rarely used them. On the principle that hay was cheaper than gas, many removed their car's motor and hitched the remaining frame to a horse. The Model T touring car at one place Murray boarded was humbled in such a way. These makeshift modes of transportation were labelled Bennett Buggies, a sad symbol of Prime Minister R. B. Bennett's impotency in the face of the Great Depression.

Murray's long walk to school was lonely and he often wished for a little company. One day he spotted a dog watching him from the opposite hillside. For quite some time he called and whistled, trying to beckon it to him, but the dog refused to come. That night at supper he was surprised when his description of the encounter sparked raucous laughter. Between hoots of mirth he was informed that he had been courting the company of a coyote!

The Ross Creek had a personality all its own. Every spring it flooded; by August it was bone dry. What happened in between was anybody's guess. One June Murray went swimming in the very spot dry enough to hold the school picnic the following June. One spring day he crossed a quiet creek in the morning only to ford two miles (three km) of rushing, calf-deep floodwaters to get back home at night.

There were other hazards as well. In the drought-parched region severe dust and electrical storms were common. "Night after night, after long hot days, there would be these black threatening clouds and electrical displays," recalls Murray, "but never a drop of rain. What a disappointment to the farmers to watch their crops burning and then see these storms with a promise of rain and none falling." On other occasions, great black walls of blowing dust swept across the prairie, choking off the sun, struggling in the darkness to unearth everything in their path. Nothing was left untouched. When the onslaught ended thick layers of dust coated the world for as far as the eye could see.

Dust gave way to snow in winter and Murray learned to cross the prairie by snowshoe. "Usually I just cut across virgin prairie," he recalls. "But if it was snowing too hard to see, I would follow the barbed wire fences. This would lead me to school in a less direct way, adding about a mile to the journey."

The winter of 1937 brought a devastating blizzard. Drifts reached as high as some rooftops. Visibility was nil. For three days Murray couldn't even attempt to get to school. He knew not one of his twenty students would either. For every day missed, however, he lost a day's pay, so on the fourth morning he donned the snowshoes and fought his way along the fences to the school. He had only to mark the register and remain until 1:00 P.M. in order to collect his wages. While sitting at his desk planning lessons, he glanced out the window at the blowing snow and noticed several strange lumps in the field beyond the barbed wire. Intrigued, he went out to investigate. Scooping snow from the nearest mound he discovered horsehair. With a sinking heart he realized the horses belonged to Cage Green. "They had been driven by the storm up against the fence and got trapped," he relates. "Every one was smothered under the snow, and there were fourteen of them. It was a sad sight to see the men digging them out to ship to a rendering plant. What a loss!" Ten days passed before roads and trails were cleared enough for students to return to school. Each day Murray struggled along the fences and back in order not to miss his pay.

In those days of dust storms and blizzards, floods and drought, poverty and loss, there was little recourse but to forge ahead, looking steadily to the future for hope and security. In 1938 Murray received just such an opportunity. It was an unimaginable step up for him to take a position near Gem in a four-room school complete with teacherage and its own water system!

On a hot July day Murray visited Abelein School for the last time. Not a sound or soul for miles around the solitary building witnessed his goodbyes. In the empty, silent schoolyard he built a bonfire to dispose of old materials. The flames turned to ashes the physical evidence of his first four years' teaching. But in the embers glowed memories not easily extinguished. Little did he consider that one day, memories such as these would be all that remained of the one-room school and the incredible era of the Dirty Thirties.

The Position

· ·
· · · · · · · ·

THE DEVASTATING ECONOMIC depression of the
1930s began in 1929 when the stock market
crash and collapse of world trade clamped Canada firmly
into the jaws of penury. Alberta and Saskatchewan, almost
entirely dependent upon wheat exports, were hit hard.
When a plethora of natural disasters, including drought,
rust, smut, army worms, cutworms, grasshoppers, relentless wind, and hailstorms tormented areas of these
provinces, a crushing double blow was struck to agrarian
populations. Thousands of farms were lost or abandoned.
Unemployment rose drastically. Even those who managed
to keep jobs saw wages steadily cut as their employers
struggled to stay in business.

The consequences of the depression filtered down to
every segment of society and rural schoolteachers were no
exception. At that time, children were legally required to
attend school until at least fifteen. A single teacher instructing up to eleven grades in one room served country schools.
Districts were approximately four miles (6.5 km) square.
Enrollments in each of their little schools varied widely,
ranging from five students to over forty, depending upon
the population of the district. As people began to leave the

prairies in search of greener pastures elsewhere rural populations plummeted, forcing the closure of many schools. With the exception of a few in newly settled areas to the north, school construction ceased almost entirely. At the same time, many high school graduates couldn't afford to attend university and were choosing instead the cheaper, more expedient route of Normal School, a postsecondary institution that trained fully qualified teachers in one year. The result was a vast surplus of teachers coupled with a dwindling number of schools. Rare job openings generated hundreds of applications each, leaving school boards besieged and bewildered. The task of narrowing down the applicants to a select dozen or so was prohibitive. From there trustees were known to flip coins, play eenie meenie minie moe, and use other unorthodox methods to make their final choice. Some even took bribes—perhaps a first month's paycheque turned back to the board. It was a real feat for any teacher, especially if fresh out of Normal School, to land a position.

. . . .

"I went to Normal School in Moose Jaw graduating in 1930. I substituted for a friend for a month in a rural school near Tuxford, Saskatchewan. It seemed as though I wrote thousands of applications before I, at last, got my own school in February 1934."

Anne Westgard (nee Benell)
Weetslade School, Saskatchewan

. . . .

"My teaching career began in 1931. That was the year teachers were a dime a dozen. I wrote applications to school boards all over the province of Alberta. Finally I was called to attend an interview with a rural school board about twenty-five miles [forty km] away from my home. There I learned that they drew straws between another applicant and me, and I was the lucky one."

Dorothy Howarth (nee Gaetz)

. . . .

"It was almost impossible to get a job teaching without experience. I applied at a rural school in central Alberta. The chairman of the school board wondered if my father could pay twenty-five dollars a month for my room and board, as the previous year the teacher had taken turns boarding with different farmers 'and this was rather inconvenient for the farmers and so this year there was a couple where she could board if her father would pay twenty-five dollars a month, for the teaching year.'"

Madeline Bailey (nee Chapman)

. . . .

"I applied for seventy-five schools and only got one by knowing a teacher who had decided to give up her school. I applied before the school trustees even advertised it. I went to see them and was accepted."

Ruth Cowan (nee Hawkins)

. . . .

"I got the position at Wealthy, north of Mannville, because my uncle filled a position on the three member school board."

Olga Allison (nee Burch)
Wealthy School, Alberta

. . . .

"It was south of Dorothy, just east of the Red Deer River. I got the job because I could ride horseback. I had to ensure that a little girl of about seven years got to school safely—up a coulee from the Red Deer River."

Dorothea Laing (nee Dove)
Cliffdale School, Alberta

. . . .

"I wrote reams of resumes and my father took me to probably every school within a radius of fifty miles [eighty km] of Killam, Alberta, my home. Luck was against me. The first question asked was what experience I had. I was new at the game and looking, so thereby was created the circle: No experience, no hiring. No hiring, no experience. I finally wrote to Mr. Sullivan at Camrose, who was the school inspector for our territory. I explained my dilemma: I had a government loan coming due in January 1933, and no prospects. Can you help me? My reply came as he arrived at our home. He had inspected at the rural school between Killam and Viking. The teacher was resigning at Christmas to get married. Immediately I made a personal application and was successful in getting employed."

Ruth Powell (nee Caldwell)
Alice Hill School, Alberta

. . . .

*"After graduating from Calgary Normal in 1931, with a
First Class Certificate, I was unable to get a school after
writing 359 applications. Without experience, I hadn't
a chance. I went back to school to take some business
courses and do some substitute teaching in Lethbridge
to gain experience. Now, with a certificate allowing me
to teach all grades up to and including grade twelve, I
began a career in a one-room school."*

Hazel McKenzie (nee Watson)
Ridgeway School, Alberta

. . . .

Teachers were indeed lucky to find a position in the
decade known as the Dirty Thirties. Sadly, many Normal
School graduates didn't, and never did use their training.
Those who were successful found their challenges far from
over. Wages were a big issue and fluctuated wildly accord-
ing to the economic status of the district. At the beginning
of the depression average annual wages were $1076 in
Saskatchewan and $1055 in Alberta. By 1932 they dropped
to $841 in Alberta and, by 1935, to $476 in Saskatchewan.
Eventually a minimum wage of $840 per year was estab-
lished in Alberta. However, if a school district could prove
it was unable to come up with the funds, it was authorized
to pay less. Many teachers received far less, and some nothing at all. They left positions with only an I.O.U. or a
promissory note to show for wages.

. . . .

"My salary in 1929/30 was ninety dollars per month, but after the first year dropped to fifty dollars."

Olga Allison (nee Burch)
Wealthy School, Alberta

. . . .

"The Dirty Thirties were just beginning and I really thought I was getting somewhere as I was earning one hundred dollars a month. Unfortunately, that didn't last. At first I had about nineteen students but that changed when people came from the dried out areas to settle on some available land. The school population jumped to nearly forty pupils. They had to do some remodelling to fit us all in. At the same time my paycheque went down to $80 and finally disappeared in my third year there. I got enough money to go home for Christmas and then that was that. I didn't pay my landlady but she managed to feed me anyway. I left there in April of my third year as my father was very ill and mother had to cope with a small market garden and a jersey cow. I stayed at home for a year and small amounts of money came from the government grants over that time until I was paid off."

Ruth Cowan (nee Hawkins)

. . . .

"I was hired in 1930 at a salary of $1050 per year or ten months, but that was only on paper. My first paycheque came while I was attending a Teachers Convention and on presenting it at the local bank it was stamped NSF. I had already rented a hotel room but a good friend and fellow teacher loaned me money to cover all the convention

expenses. Later I learned that the teacher who preceded me had garnisheed my wages. Consequently it was nearly Christmas before I received any wages and by that time my salary had been cut to $840 per annum. Fortunately my parents helped me and I was able to pay my landlady a dollar a day board and room."

Camilla Cline (nee Kilborn)
Ribstone Creek School, Alberta

. . . .

"One year during my four and a half year stay there, a member of the board instigated to reduce my salary from $840 to $750 for the year, on the basis that if the neighbouring school only paid $750, then they should follow suit. This only happened for one year and with a change in board members, the new member said, 'We can pay $840 and we will.' At that time with jobs scarce and teachers plentiful one did not argue."

Ruth Powell (nee Caldwell)
Alice Hill School, Alberta

. . . .

"My salary was seven hundred dollars per year but it was not all paid until the large divisions were formed. The grant from the government was divided among the previous teachers, the present teacher receiving the larger share."

Helena Brown
Preston Lake School, Alberta

. . . .

"My salary was seven hundred dollars per annum—
but I frequently received only twenty-five dollars per
month to pay my room and board. When I went home
for Christmas I had to borrow money from my father
for transportation and hotel accommodation."

Madeline Bailey (nee Chapman)
Gillion School, Alberta

. . . .

As the depression wore on salaries were further reduced. In 1938, Ed Redecopp sent out fifty thoughtfully written and entirely fruitless applications before hearing of an available school fifty miles from his Saskatchewan home. This time he borrowed his father's Oldsmobile and drove the distance to apply to the school board in person. He was informed that another applicant had offered to teach for a paltry $250 a year. Desperate for work, Ed countered with two hundred dollars and was instantly hired. He received a paycheque of ten dollars a month and a promissory note for one hundred dollars at the end of the school year.

A small government grant was issued to each school, but the majority of teachers' wages came from school taxes paid by the residents of the district to the school board. The increasingly impoverished rural populations were often unable to pay. Many teachers waited months before enough tax money could be scratched up to meet their due.

. . . .

"It was the worst years of the depression. Taxes for the upkeep of roads and schools were not paid. The government grant paid for the coal, for a small salary for the secretary and for the janitor, and if there was anything left I got a small cheque. At that time the minimum salary set by the Alberta Teachers Association was $840 for the school year of ten months. As there was no way most school boards could pay that much, most beginning teachers agreed to take less, to gain experience. I had a contract for seven hundred dollars annually, which eventually was paid. My dear father paid my room and board, twenty-five dollars a month."

Hazel McKenzie (nee Watson)
Ridgeway School, Alberta

. . . .

"I made only five hundred dollars a year, but I had a teacherage. The last year I was there the school district went broke and we were not paid from Easter until July. I charged my groceries during that time and my bill was twenty-seven dollars for the three months."

Dorothea Laing (nee Dove)
Wardlow School, Alberta

. . . .

"In 1930 I was offered a salary of one thousand dollars per year, but since we were in depression times, money soon ran out and they were going to close the school. I offered to teach for my board. They took me up on this and also found a little extra."

Mary Cooke (nee Sanderson)
Cresco School, Saskatchewan

. . . .

*"In 1937 my salary was $350 for the year, but I didn't
get much of it until later, and my mother sent me money
for stamps and the necessities."*

Agnes Hunter (nee Burnett)

. . . .

*"In 1935 I earned four hundred dollars a year, did the
janitor work, built the fire. This was all very new to me—
a city girl. But I managed and the second year I was
there the Social Credit government had come in and my
salary was raised to five hundred dollars."*

Ruth Keiver (nee Coffin)
Benton Valley School, Alberta

. . . .

Even when teachers knew the money was there, actu-
ally laying hands on it wasn't always easy.

. . . .

*"I started teaching in 1930 with a salary of one thousand
dollars per year. As the depression dragged on, my salary
was eventually reduced to six hundred dollars per year. My
paycheque was never mailed to me. On payday I saddled
my faithful horse and rode to the home of the secretary-
treasurer. He gave me the signed cheque for the month.
I continued on to the home of the chairman of the school
board to get his signature on the cheque. Every month my
saddle horse took me over this ten mile route."*

Lillian Coulson (nee Thompson)

. . . .

"I had such a hard time to get hold of my cheque as an old farmer was the only one on the school board. I was desperate one time and walked to his place to get my cheque. I was met by a vicious dog who bit my leg as I was running home. I stopped at a neighbour's place and a kind lady washed and wrapped up my leg so I could get home. I never tried that trick again."

Evelyn Hardy
Anthony Hill School, Alberta

. . . .

On at least one occasion, Nettie Smith didn't have to worry about such things as signatures and tracking down her paycheque. She and her husband rented farmland in southern Alberta, but because of drought and crop failure they were dependent upon Nettie's teaching for their livelihood. Because of this she was one of the few married women allowed to teach during the thirties. When the trustees of her school fell two months behind on her salary, with still no cash to give her, they deemed it fair to compensate her with two cows instead!

Jessie's Story

· ·
· · · · · · · ·

FROM 1936 TO 39 "home" for Jessie Bissell (now Rollings) was the two cloakrooms of the Silver Fox School. Two minuscule rooms divided by a hallway. One served as a kitchen–livingroom furnished with a tiny table, two chairs, coal oil lamp, and a few cooking and eating utensils. A small, wood-fuelled airtight heater provided warmth; fitted into its stovepipe was a miniature oven. Until Jessie learned to manipulate the draft that controlled the oven's temperature, she endured undercooked, overcooked, and downright burnt meals.

Across the hall, the other room had no heat and made an ideal cold storage room eight months a year. Equipped with a hide-a-bed sofa, it also served as Jessie's bedroom.

Jessie was pleased to accept these conditions. After sending out countless applications, the Edmonton Normal School graduate was thrilled to finally obtain a school only eighteen miles (twenty-nine km) from her home town of Athabasca, Alberta.

With her father's help she moved a few essential belongings and a supply of food to her new home. The journey was made tedious by the miles of muskeg that lay between Athabasca and the Silver Fox district. Jessie and her father travelled many extra miles to skirt the grassy bogs.

Despite her entitlement to the minimum $840 a year, Jessie signed a contract for five hundred dollars. By doing so she became the sixth teacher to whom the school board owed money. Many residents couldn't pay their school taxes; many more were in arrears. It wasn't until October 31, when she should have had one hundred dollars coming, that Jessie received a token sum of fifteen dollars. Nearly two months later she received twenty-five dollars. Twenty-five dollars a month thereafter brought her a grand total of $190 by the end of her first teaching year.

In addition to receiving far less money than promised, Jessie had to begin teaching a week before the start of her first term. This was to make up the previous year's quota of two hundred teaching days. If not met, no government grant would be issued. Jessie willingly obliged.

She had forty-nine students in nine grades. Her schoolroom, like many, reflected the cultural diversity of the prairies. There were coloured students who had moved to Silver Fox from the African-American settlement in the neighbouring Amber Valley. There were Danish, German, Metis, and Ukrainian students as well. Some beginners couldn't speak English. Jessie needed to keep her wits about her while becoming a master of organization and efficiency. There wasn't a moment wasted. Older students were indispensable with the youngsters, listening to them read, helping with their spelling, and drilling them on times tables. After school Jessie gave extra time to grade nine students; they would be required to write departmental exams in June. "The chairman of the board handed me a strip of threshing machine belt—my strap—and said, 'use it!'" There was little need.

Not a solitary book graced the school's library shelves, not even a dictionary. The board supplied readers, but arithmetic books and spellers were often hand-me-downs. The large wall clock worked, but was unreliable because few people had watches or radios by which to set it. Ink for straight pens and nibs was made by dissolving blue ink tablets in water. It often froze on cold winter nights, bursting the glass inkwells on each desk.

Meagre though it was, Jessie drew on her December paycheque for supplies to make a hectograph, yesteryear's precursor to the modern-day photocopier. A can of French gelatin, cookie sheet, and purple hectograph pencil were all she needed. She melted the gelatin to pouring consistency by placing the can in hot water. Then she poured it into the cookie sheet and allowed it to cool and solidify. With the purple hectograph pencil she wrote master copies of exams and seatwork. By wetting the surface of the gelatin in the cookie sheet with water, then laying her master copy face down upon it, she transferred her writing on to the gelatin. Then it was simply a matter of smoothing additional sheets of paper, one at a time, over the transfer to make extra copies of the same work. Although messy and time consuming, the hectograph was state-of-the-art equipment in the thirties and saved Jessie copious amounts of writing.

Jessie carried water for her own use from the closest neighbour, a quarter mile south. The school's water arrived with the students. It was kept in a tin pail on a bench with a community dipper above it. Close by was a single wash basin and roller towel. Once a week the students took turns taking the towel home for badly needed washing.

The Silver Fox district couldn't afford the standard Quebec or Waterbury heater recommended for one-room schoolhouses. Instead they made do with a large gas barrel turned on its side, fitted with strap-iron legs, a door in one end, and a hole in the top for a stovepipe. In exchange for partial relief from mounting tax burdens, farmers supplied cordwood for fuel. "It was slow to start," says Jessie, "but gave off a good heat as the day wore on."

Like Murray's, Jessie's students began classes on cold mornings with their desks pushed into a semicircle around the stove. After school, Jessie opened the cloakroom doors to allow the heat to seep into her miniature quarters.

During recess the children enjoyed many games. Their favourite was softball. The school board usually issued one ball and one bat per year, but in the fall of 1936 substitutes had to suffice. A mushy, stringy, flat ball was all that was available. The students unwound it, rewound it with string, binder twine and strips of rag, and replaced the much-mended cover. A bat was fashioned by whittling down a board—and in Jessie's words, "The game was on!"

A more gruesome but practical activity involved hunting rabbits. At four cents apiece, rabbit pelts were a ready source of cash in hard times. Often the children caught and killed the rabbits with sticks, then skinned them on the spot. At home, many of their porches and entranceways were lined with rows of drying skins.

Winter months brought bone chilling cold, but the children continued their outdoor amusements. Building snowmen, digging tunnels, making angels, and playing snow games took the forefront. "Containers of cocoa placed on the tin rack on the barrel stove at recess provided a hot drink," recalls Jessie. Unfortunately, one day a little one forgot to remove the lid from his can and it exploded, spraying hot chocolate all over the ceiling.

The next year a new arrangement was devised. Three days a week students took turns bringing soup bones, vegetables, and other ingredients to school, and a kind-hearted lady living nearby made soup for noon lunches. The other two days Jessie made hot cocoa on her own stove. These lovely, warming drinks went a long way towards compensating for the frozen sandwiches in lard pail lunch buckets.

"Most of the children walked to school," remembers Jessie. "Some rode horseback, came by buggy in summer, or cutter in winter, or dog team, or the more comfortable caboose, which was prone to upset on snow drifted roads."

A cutter was a small, lightweight sleigh. A caboose was a closed-in cutter, much like the one Robert Kroetsch (as he relates in his prologue), managed to destroy three times. These conveyances were precariously balanced even when roads were good, but where Jessie lived roads weren't maintained. Eventually drifts grew so big that the smaller students had trouble negotiating them even on foot. When they became impossible for two of the youngest girls, they stayed over at the school with Jessie, no doubt delighted to enjoy a little holiday with "Teacher."

Jessie walked one and a half miles (2.5 km) to pick up her mail from the private home that doubled as the district's post office. One day as she returned a blizzard blew in, the swirling drifting snow building up so quickly she could hardly make her way through it. Wisely, she stopped at the nearest farm to wait out the storm. The couple living there wouldn't hear of her venturing out again and insisted she spend the night. Jessie shared their only bed with the wife while the husband slept downstairs on the couch.

Jessie was warmly appreciative of this kindness. She was learning, however, that generosity was typical of the people of the Silver Fox district.

Another stormy weekend Jessie discovered her food supply was very low. All she had left was one egg, a small amount of flour, and some ketchup. It seemed impossible to fashion an adequate meal out of such ingredients. She remembered, however, that a parent had shown her how to make noodles. She combined the egg and flour, shaped and cooked the noodles, and seasoned the tender results with ketchup. A very acceptable meal!

On Monday morning a student surprised her by bringing in groceries and coal oil. The chairman of the school board, knowing she was low on supplies, had hazarded the snowed-in roads to town himself, in order to replenish her stocks.

Spring arrived swarming with caterpillars. "Trees, grass, road, and buildings were coated with the seething, moving mass," recalls Jessie. The poplar trees surrounding the school were a favourite feasting spot; they literally dripped with the loathsome creatures. Like creeping ivy the bristled larvae edged their way up the school walls. To the boys' delight and the girls' horror they slowly advanced over the step and through the door. Jessie swept them like dirt right back out again. Then one day, as quickly as they came, the caterpillars vanished, cocooning themselves away to await winged rebirth.

While hordes of caterpillars occupied the land, vast numbers of fish crowded the rivers, surging upstream to spawn their young. So dense were they that men, women, and boys, shod in rubber boots, waded into the swirling melee and tossed fish by the pitchfork-full back to land.

This abundant harvest of fish was then canned or layered with salt in barrels for later eating.

In June 1939, King George VI and his consort, Queen Elizabeth, were crossing Canada on a royal tour of the nation. Excitement reigned supreme! Everyone craved an opportunity to glimpse the revered couple. Jessie's students were no exception. They arranged for a farm truck to take them to the city of Edmonton, through which the king and queen were scheduled to pass. Little did they realize as they made their excited plans that the journey would almost end in tragedy.

The night before leaving, students who lived some distance away slept on the school floor. Early next morning everybody, including some parents, jammed into the back of the truck and set off over gravel roads for Edmonton. The trip was long and dusty, but the atmosphere was jovial. Some of the travellers had never been to the city before.

They arrived to thousands of people thronging Kingsway Avenue in anticipation of the royal couple's approach. Jessie's group found a place for themselves on the bleachers raised for the occasion, then settled in to await the magic. They weren't disappointed. As the monarchs drove slowly by the crowds cheered wildly. Everyone was struck by the graciousness of their royal highnesses who gazed benevolently upon the crowd, smiling and waving. Many were convinced that the queen looked right at them, personally. It was a brief moment in time, made precious for a lifetime. Afterwards people bought souvenirs, ate the lunches they had packed along, and watched fireworks. It was a long, gratifying day.

The air was cool as the Silver Fox group piled into their

farm truck for the long trip home. Tired but happy, they huddled into a knot to keep warm. The ride was bumpy, but they were used to that. With everyone hunched together, nobody bothered to peer over the high sides of the box. Suddenly, a massive jolt sent bodies flying through the air. It happened so quickly that they were all on the ground before realizing they had even left the truck. After a stunned moment, a cacophony of crying and screaming rose from the darkness. It was sheer fright. Exhausted, the driver had fallen asleep, and the truck had slowly left the road, descending the slope toward the treacherously rushing Tawatinaw Creek. Just feet from the torrent it overturned, spilling its human cargo. A garageman from the nearby town of Rochester helped the shaken lot upright their truck. If they had not all been huddled so tightly together for warmth, he said, they would surely have suffered serious injury. "No one was even scratched," marvels Jessie.

The Sports Day at the end of term was another highlight. It always took place on the last day of school. The entire district participated. Three-legged races, sack races, Egg on Spoon, and Thread the Needle were just some of the fast and furious games played. A superb lunch was provided by the ladies, after which young and old alike played softball.

While all this activity took place two large ice cream freezers occupied positions of honour in the shade. Canisters of whole cream and other ingredients, tucked into buckets of ice and coarse salt, were churned continuously until the cream froze. The job took hours, and required many hands to take turns chipping the ice from large blocks, turning the canister cranks and scraping down the cream. The results were well worth it. Ice cream in depression era rural areas, where refrigeration was nonexistent, was a rare and cherished treat. After the games and ice cream, farm families reluctantly straggled home to chores, then returned with renewed exuberance to see the school year out by dancing until the crack of dawn.

Jessie never forgot the people of the Silver Fox school district. In September of 1939 she obtained another school just five miles (eight km) from her home. This time she boarded in a real house, was able to walk home on weekends, and received forty-four dollars a month like clockwork. "There were twenty books in the library," she recalls, "an easy chair, and a well." Things had definitely improved! Despite all this, the kindness and good times Jessie experienced at the Silver Fox School remained golden treasures, preserved forever in the special places of her heart.

Accommodation

DURING THE THIRTIES, rural teachers in general lived in small teacherages on or near the school grounds, or in the homes of area residents on a room and board basis. As in Jessie's case, a few even lived in the school itself. These situations were new and challenging experiences for the young pedagogue, often not only from the city, but also living on his or her own for the first time. The poverty and discomfort inflicted by the depression and lack of modern conveniences made conditions harsh. Perhaps they were also what made people so determined to be as friendly and accommodating as possible. For the most part the highly esteemed teacher was welcomed throughout the district. In time he or she learned to accept less than ideal living conditions and focus instead on the pleasures of friends and social activities.

"I was lucky to have a good place to live with nice people. My bedroom in the small house was an added on lean-to open to the winds on three sides. Two windows without storm windows or screens let snow drift onto my pillow.

There was no basement under it and it was separated from the kitchen by a storage room, so that no heat penetrated. Water in the wash basin and jug froze and the linoleum floor was icy. I learned to get dressed under the bedclothes. But the meals were excellent and the family [members] have remained good friends."

Hazel McKenzie (nee Watson)
Ridgeway School, Alberta

. . . .

Frigid accommodation was common. Houses were generally only heated by coal and wood burning kitchen ranges, which were banked up at night in an effort to conserve the dying heat. It was impossible for warmth to infiltrate every corner of the house, especially if it was two storeys high. During the winter it was standard to sleep in subzero temperatures, and there were other discomforts as well.

. . . .

"During January and February, our coldest months, my little 'shack' was cold. Water froze every night. Luckily, I did not freeze under a featherdown comforter. I did suffer from chilblains as my feet were constantly cold."

Annie Tym (nee Sankey)
Pleasant Heights School, Alberta

. . . .

"My upstairs bedroom was cold in the winter. Many times I broke the ice in the water pitcher to wash in the morning —a real wake up experience, believe me! They tried to keep out wind drafts by packing rags around the window frame, and Grace, the eleven-year-old daughter, a warm sleeper, slept with me to help keep me warm on cold nights. However, there was an epidemic of the ITCH throughout the area and consequently I got it too. Frantically I hurried to the doctor. It was a stubborn thing to contend with."

Hazel Youngs (nee Ray)
Longsdale School, Alberta

. . . .

"The first year I boarded with a family who lived two and a half miles [four km] from school. This house was old and very cold. On winter mornings the blankets would have white frost on them from my breath during the night. It housed lots of mice, too, and they chewed out a large piece of cloth from my new coat to make a nest for their babies."

Camilla Cline (nee Kilborn)
Rough Meadow School, Alberta

. . . .

"First I had to find a boarding place—the family that boarded the former teacher had moved away. Yes, this family, husband, wife, and three little ones would board me. They put me in an unused spare room upstairs in their old log house. Log houses in those days were inclined to have bed bugs. I was attacked that first night.

*They came out of the cracks to sample my rich red blood,
which showed signs of spillage as I swatted them in my
sleep on my nightwear. The following nights weren't bad,
as the bed and mattress had been thoroughly cleansed
with coal oil. They were put to route but the odour of coal
oil lingered on."*

Ruby Hughes (nee Scott)
Golden Sheaf School, Alberta

. . . .

Many teachers who boarded weren't lucky enough to
be given a bedroom of their own. Farmhouses of just two
or three rooms were the norm, as were relatively large
families.

. . . .

*"There were five children in the family. I shared a bed
with the oldest girl."*

Margaret Briggs (nee Dams)
Shady Lane School, Alberta

. . . .

*"At Hillmartin School I boarded with the George Brown
family who had a teenage daughter not much younger
than I was. She and I shared a room. Their small house
had only two bedrooms."*

Jessie Pendergast (nee Erskine)
Hillmartin School, Alberta

. . . .

"At one place I was given the only bedroom, which I shared with a ten-year-old girl."

Agnes Hunter (nee Burnett)

. . . .

People were deplorably poor. Due to abysmal crop failures and record low prices for wheat, sixty-six percent of Saskatchewan's rural population were forced onto government relief. Alberta was not far behind. The problem of collecting enough school taxes to pay the teacher was critical. Some enterprising districts found a way around this. Their teachers were asked to board for a period of time at each home in the district. Room and board was deducted from their paycheque, while an equivalent amount was deducted from the farmer's taxes owing. This enabled the school board to pay part of the teacher's salary, the teacher to pay room and board, and every farmer in the district to pay some of his taxes with no money ever changing hands.

. . . .

"I was to board around and each family had fifteen dollars deducted from their taxes. I was also allowed some relief money, $7.95, I believe. This was given to the people where I boarded for groceries."

Agnes Hunter (nee Burnett)

. . . .

With no electricity, coal oil lamps provided dim light in the evenings. Each morning their bowls were refilled, wicks trimmed, and globes washed in preparation for the next evening. Butter and milk were kept fresh in the cellar or well and eggs were preserved for months in water glass, a sodium silicate solution. Flour was stored in the attic. There was a knack to piling it so the mice wouldn't get into it. The only time fresh meat was available was after a cow or pig was butchered. Otherwise meat was canned, pickled, smoked, or salted and put in crocks. Some farmers raised chickens.

. . . .

"We were seven miles from town with no refrigeration and meat was expensive. They raised chickens and we had a lot of chicken dinners, and eggs! The hens were running out on grass and the egg yolks were dark and strong. She cooked them in every way possible, poached, fried, scrambled, devilled—but still it was years before I could look an egg in the eye again."

Hazel Youngs (nee Ray)
Longsdale School, Alberta

. . . .

Water had to be hauled in. It was heated on the wood stove for washing purposes. Clothes were scrubbed on a washboard. Bathing occurred once a week and consisted of little more than a sponge bath, or perhaps, if one was lucky, a few inches of water in the bottom of a galvanized tub. As the heat, wind, and lack of rain gradually dried up wells, sloughs and lakes, farmers went farther and farther afield to find water. The precious substance had to be strictly rationed. The same water used for bathing might then be used for scrubbing clothes, then for washing floors, and so on.

. . . .

"At my first boarding place I was allotted part of a large pitcher of water for a week. A large matching bowl was my sink. One day I washed a pair of cotton hose, the only kind we had in those days. Maybe I did a few other things I was not to do so I was asked to move."

Jeana Stanford (nee Russell)
Montpelier School, Alberta

. . . .

One thing for which water wasn't required was the bathroom: an outdoor biffy (small shed) placed over a large hole well away from the house. One or two circular openings in a wooden ledge over the trench made seats. No flushing was required. Sheets torn from an old catalogue, and the occasional luxury of tissues from Christmas oranges, provided toilet paper. These "conveniences" were smelly and fly-infested in the summer. In the winter snow drifted in, sometimes as high as the bench, and the seat was coated with ice. Hence, trips to the "outhouse" became as few and far between as possible.

. . . .

"The outdoor privy was conveniently located behind the house in a grove of trees, lovely in summer but the snow invaded it in the winter. A sheet or two from the catalogue hanging nearby was always used to wipe the snow from the seat before settling down."

> Camilla Cline (nee Kilborn)
> Ribstone Creek School, Alberta

. . . .

Buying new clothing was an extravagance few, including teachers, could afford. Mothers patched and repatched worn clothes, cladding children literally in rags. Some households didn't have enough clothing for all the children to attend school, so siblings took turns wearing the same clothes, only attending when it was their day. There was no such thing as a school dress code. One dress could last a week by wearing it front to back the first and second day, back to front the third and fourth day, and inside out the fifth.

Teachers often had only one or two outfits to work in.

. . . .

"I darned and redarned my cotton stockings, and my winter wardrobe consisted of two wool knitted suits, a red one and a green one. One week I would wear the red one to school and save the green one for the dance on Friday night. The next week I wore the green one to

school. When the elbows wore thin, I took out the sleeves, put them in the opposite armholes and was ready for the next week."

Agnes Hunter (nee Burnett)

. . . .

In mild weather most children went barefoot. In cold weather a single pair of shoes, stuffed with rags, created a custom fit for every child in the house. When shoes wore out completely, parents fashioned footwear from anything sturdy and handy—car tires and canvas, for instance. Woolen socks made good mittens. Cayenne pepper, sprinkled into stockings, gave at least the illusion of keeping feet warmer.

. . . .

"In those days mothers made clothes from hand-me-downs, worn blankets, flour and sugar sacks, or rolled oat sacks. Toques, mitts, and socks were knit from old garments that had been ravelled and rewound. Often cow or horse hides were home-tanned and made into mitts and moccasins. These were also used as bed blankets. One family used rabbit skins for bedding. They were warm but the fur stuck to everything and it wasn't easy to brush off."

Camilla Cline (nee Kilborn)
Rough Meadow School, Alberta

. . . .

The family lucky enough to own a radio often couldn't use it. Batteries were too expensive to replace. Likewise, most people owned telephones that had been disconnected to avoid the monthly charge. Communication was difficult. Some regions had an ingenious way of getting around this problem.

. . . .

"The men decided to have their own system. Using the barbed wire fences as telephone lines, and with old radio handspeakers and earphones, they could talk to nearby farms. There was usually one family who still had a proper phone who would contact the operator in Carmangay to tell of any news or happenings of interest or importance. She would relay it to someone in each district who used the fence phone to spread the news."

Hazel McKenzie (nee Watson)
Ridgeway School, Alberta

. . . .

In areas of severe drought vegetable gardens couldn't survive unless watered by hand. In some regions water was so limited that gardens had to be allowed to die. People couldn't afford to buy vegetables, so went without, adding nutritional poverty to material poverty. Russian thistle, commonly known as tumbleweed, grew in abundance and was experimented with for greens. The results were vile and often discarded. Occasionally peddlers from British Columbia appeared, bartering fruit for horse and cattle hides or chickens. Wheat or barley was roasted or ground into a coffee substitute. Whole wheat, boiled into porridge, suffered such additives as potatoes, raisins, onions, and even weeds, to boost nutritional value. Some families subsisted entirely on potatoes and skim milk. For others, jackrabbit or gopher meat, made into stews and pies, was common fare.

When people in eastern Canada heard how their western neighbours suffered, they organized a massive campaign to help bring relief. Dozens of freight cars full of goods arrived on the prairies. Clothing, tinned fruit, fresh apples, dried beans, and turnips were just some of the offerings. The salted cod that came from the Maritimes in flat stacks tied with twine was a mystery to the prairie people. They didn't know how to cook it and much of it went to waste.

. . . .

"It was during this time that the government sent food to help the people. They received salted fish, cheese, dried herrings. Children brought the herrings to school in their pockets. The first night they got the fish Alice cooked one. There were no taps in those days. Between supper and bedtime three of us drank one pail of water. After that Alice soaked the fish first."

Jeana Stanford (nee Russell)
Sherburne School, Alberta

. . . .

Boarding in a strange home required adjustment on the part of everyone. Some situations were positive, others negative. For the most part, people went out of their way to make the teacher comfortable. Teachers helped on the farm whenever they could and it was generally assumed they'd participate in all the family activities.

. . . .

"I was invited into a home just a mile [1.6 km] from the school and here I stayed until the end of my teaching days at Rough Meadow. It was a wonderful home to live in and I was accepted as a family member and treated as such. I always called her my 'Second Mother' and she well deserved the title. I remember one morning I started out for school but by the time I had reached the road I realized I had forgotten something so I went back for it. She was horrified and told me to sit up on the table, swing my feet and count to twenty. That would remove the curse of my having to return and would guarantee that my day at school would be pleasant."

Camilla Cline (nee Kilborn)
Rough Meadow School, Alberta

. . . .

"As time went on I began to appreciate the generosity and friendliness of these people. They willingly shared their activities, their horses, and their homes. For instance, at one home the thoughtful landlady put a hot water bottle in my bed when I was out to the school dances on cold Friday nights."

Agnes Hunter (nee Burnett)

. . . .

"The next year I boarded a mile from school with a younger couple. I paid thirty dollars a month and it was worth every cent. I enjoyed myself so much with them, even if I just had eight dollars at the end of the month."

Evelyn Hardy
Anthony Hill School, Alberta

. . . .

"I paid thirty-five dollars a month for board. I had a good place to stay. It was a house built by an Englishman who had bought a ranch of many thousands of acres. He had built a house with a servant's pantry between the kitchen and the dining room. The people I stayed with were the caretakers."

Dorothea Laing (nee Dove)
Cliffdale School, Alberta

. . . .

"I was lucky in that I paid only seventeen dollars a month, the food was great, and I had a horse to ride or drive to school, a distance of two miles [three km], when I so desired."

Muriel Lugg (nee Smith)
Fidelity School, Alberta

. . . .

"I was welcomed throughout the house and many hours were spent playing cards and games. There was also a piano, which I was welcome to play."

Hazel Youngs (nee Ray)
Longsdale School, Alberta

. . . .

"I was to find my own boarding place, which I did at Mrs. Marry Harris' for eighteen dollars a month. The accommodation was excellent, although I walked two miles [three km] to school. The wee house out back was very familiar and no electricity or water on the tap. I only boarded at Mrs. Harris' until June. Due to a nasty fall on snow covered ice while walking to school I tried to find a closer boarding place. I was successful and found a place a quarter mile [half a km] from the school where I stayed for two years until they needed the room due to increased family, so I moved again. Although I was four miles [6.5 km] from school, two miles [three km] if I followed the fences, I was happily situated. My brother lent me his horse to ride to school for the last year I taught there. I had a beautiful room, wonderful accommodation. I made lifetime friends with the family."

Ruth Powell (nee Caldwell)
Alice Hill School, Alberta

. . . .

A certain amount of politicking accompanied the boarding of the teacher. Some felt having the teacher raised their status in the district. Others didn't want anything to do with it. Inevitably, the teacher was the one caught in the middle.

. . . .

"My landlady was very defensive about boarding the teacher and made sure no one could accuse her of grabbing the profits. Teachers were 'free to board where they wished.' She wasn't going to put up lunches or wait on anyone. They'd have to look after themselves, even to the point of emptying their own bedchamber—a tricky task since one had to carry it through the kitchen to the outdoors and there were three men besides the school children to avoid."

Hazel Youngs (nee Ray)
Longsdale School, Alberta

. . . .

The alternative to boarding was living in a teacherage, if one was available. This was ideally (but not always) a one- or two-room house built near the school and equipped with some basic rudiments. Enjoyed by some, dreaded by others, the teacherage experience was never forgotten.

. . . .

"I boarded with a family who lived about a mile and a half [2.5 km] from the school. The second year she didn't want the teacher anymore and no other home wanted a boarder so they built a small teacherage on the school ground. Well, I did the best I could, but living alone was not for me. I was scared every night. I bought a Model A and went home weekends to Calgary and whenever I could get anyone to come and stay with me I was so happy."

Ruth Keiver (nee Coffin)
New Valley School, Alberta

. . . .

"Towards the end of September Inspector Liggett came. He was pleased but felt that my boarding place, three and a half miles away [5.5 km], was too far from school. If I worked after school, then I had to walk back all the way. The inspector was concerned and most helpful. He approached the school board to bring in a small shack, which they did. It gave me a far better opportunity to work in the classroom after school and early in the morning."

Annie Tym (nee Sankey)
Pleasant Heights School, Alberta

. . . .

"[At my boarding place] one evening . . . the husband remarked that I might find the mile and a half [2.5 km] walk to school rather cold with winter coming on and they didn't have a spare saddle horse, so how would I like to move into the old teacherage? It was right on the school ground and of course it would be all fixed up as new.

In October I moved into the teacherage . . . [a] frame, one storey, one room house with a lean to shed stocked with wood and coal for the small, four-burner cooking stove. There was a double bed with a spring that sagged in the middle, also a table and plenty of cupboards with pots and pans. I supplied my own bedding. The walls were freshly painted with pale blue kalsomine. The only relief from blue was when the sparkling frost, during a cold spell, shone in the corners of the room. I was afraid to bank the stove too full even with the drafts shut, as I wasn't taking any chances on fire.

A family who lived two miles [three km] from school allowed their eleven-year-old, Alice, to keep me company during the week, as I was a bit nervous of being alone on the bald headed prairie at night, especially when the coyotes howled.

There was no well on the property. The water for school and household use was brought to us in cream cans, when we needed it. Dishes, hands and faces, and tea once a day took up most of our water.

As the weather became colder and I didn't get home every weekend . . . Annie, aged thirteen, came to stay with me, even on weekends. A mother who lived out of the school district asked me to do her a favour by taking her little boy, Jesse, to start grade one. He was only six, but this would give him a start. She would supply his cot and take him home weekends. As Jesse stayed with Annie and I, his mother was so kind in bringing us cold meats, bread, and pastries."

Ruby Hughes (nee Scott)
Golden Sheaf School, Alberta

. . . .

"I still made only five hundred dollars a year but I had a one room teacherage—outdoor plumbing. It was about twelve feet by fifteen feet [3.5 m by 4.5 m]. It had cupboards and a clothes closet. The stove was cast iron, small, possibly the top would have been twenty inches by twenty-four inches [fifty-one cm by sixty-one cm]. It burned wood and coal. I was supplied with each. I enjoyed the pupils and the people. They were very good to me. I was often invited to their homes for meals. They sent me vegetables when they were in season."

Dorothea Laing (nee Dove)
Wardlow School, Alberta

. . . .

"The last two years I taught there I lived in a converted chicken house with no modern conveniences."

Madeline Bailey (nee Chapman)
Gillion School, Alberta

. . . .

Although it couldn't legally be stated in their contracts, many teachers were also required to do the janitorial work in the school. Sometimes this was in exchange for rent and fuel. Ed Redecopp, who taught at Vendetta School in Saskatchewan in 1938, was one of these. He and his brother Jake (one of his students) lived in a one-room milk shed hauled onto the schoolgrounds by the chairman. The brothers levelled it with two by fours, plugged its numerous gaps with bits of wood and tin, and banked it up with dirt to keep out frost and wildlife. They furnished the place with cast-offs from home and found enough material from an abandoned farm nearby to build shelves. Curtains were tea towels serving double duty. The pair walked everywhere. The nearest store was a seven mile (eleven km) hike. There they bought modest supplies on Ed's ten dollar a month paycheque. They were desperately poor, but an inherent sense of humor wouldn't let them get discouraged. They opened their cans from the bottom, and placed them back on the shelves right side up when empty. This continuous appearance of a full larder bolstered their spirits, even if they hadn't a scrap to eat. Parents of Ed's school children knew better, however, and took it upon themselves to prevent the boys from starving. A steady stream of vegetables, meat, milk, soup, and baking appeared at the milk-shed door. In return, Ed and Jake helped with farm work whenever they could and Ed taught music lessons to anyone interested. Eventually they had enough aspiring musicians to form a band and began playing for dances in the district. Not only was this great entertainment, but it earned Ed and his brother much needed extra cash.

Some teachers had neither a teacherage nor a place to board. The only accommodation available for them was the school itself: the cloakrooms, the cellar, the attic, or even a corner of the classroom. This meant a very makeshift existence indeed, but for the sake of a job, many teachers were quite willing to put up with almost anything.

Perhaps Mary Cooke (nee Sanderson) had the best of both boarding and living on her own. She occupied a one-room hut built for her in a farmer's yard about half a mile from the Cresco School in Saskatchewan. It contained a single bed, a small table and chair, and a tin heater. She ate her meals in the farmhouse with the family and they were excellent company, but when she desired privacy and a quiet place to work, her snug little cabin was just footsteps away.

Murray's Story (II)

· ·
· · · · · · · ·

MURRAY ROBISON FELT like a king when, in 1938, he accepted a teaching position near Gem, Alberta. The rural four-room school with staff of five seemed palatial next to Abelein, the one-room school he had formerly served. There he had taught eight grades alone while struggling with myriad custodial chores. At the Gem Consolidated School, however, he was delighted to have an entire room for teaching just three grades, and was thrilled with the luxury of central heating and indoor chemical toilets. "I had really come up in the world," he says. "There was even a janitor to look after all the cleaning and heating and maintenance!"

Murray wasn't the only newcomer to Gem School that year. Spencer Rae, a young man Murray knew well from boyhood days in Medicine Hat, joined the staff as principal. He and Murray were offered the teacherage on the schoolgrounds. They were happy to take a stab at "baching it" together.

Setting up housekeeping was the first order of business. Sparsely furnished, the teacherage contained only a bed in each of two bedrooms, and table, chairs, and coal stove in a small kitchen. The living room stood empty and cheerless. Outside were the customary coal shed and out-house.

Spencer's family owned a hardware store in Medicine Hat, and Murray once worked at Moore's Furniture there. With the Rae Hardware truck they made a foray into Moore's second hand department and brought home some great deals. A desk table, small rug, and living room chairs rounded out their furnishings.

Murray was a camera buff. "I hung a few of my 'Photographic Masterpieces' on the walls," he chuckles, "and we were all set."

Having completed their interior decorating, the men turned their attention outdoors. The schoolyard, about four miles from the village of Gem, was surrounded by farmers' fields. Irrigation had encouraged the growth of abundant trees and acres of flowing grain, creating a pocket of beauty in the prairie desert. The teacherage itself, however, choked amid masses of mustard weed and Russian thistle. With a sense of righteous purpose, Murray and Spencer decided to eliminate the unsightly mess. "The easiest way to handle the situation," Murray recalls, "was to burn the weeds. It was autumn and they were quite dry. So, armed with two rakes and a match we set to."

The work began innocently enough, but soon the tiny flames acquired strength and greed. Possessed with a mind of their own they grew and raced toward a magnificent stand of harvest-ready wheat, just yards from the teacherage. A first class prairie fire was in the making! "Lord were we scared!" remembers Murray.

They fought frantically to control the conflagration, but their monumental efforts were matched and surpassed by the mounting flames. Not daring to succumb to exhaustion, the two men struggled desperately on with shovels and wet sacks until the terrible flames were at last quelled. Clothing singed, lungs scorched, weak from terror and exertion, the knowledge of their close escape left them trembling. High prices to pay for a weed-free yard!

Before the school year began Spencer and Murray organized the school's chemical storage closet. Most of the boxes and bottles, having lost their labels, were unrecognizable. Spencer didn't want students and staff second-guessing the contents of these mysterious packages, so he elected to dispose of them. The question was how? In those days environmental issues had yet to come to the forefront; there were no such things as toxic chemical round-ups. The two men decided to dig a pit and throw the unknown substances into it. It's unfortunate they didn't advertise their intentions, for area residents would have enjoyed the fireworks that ensued. Each chemical, as it was tossed into the pit, reacted with those that had gone before to create a new and thrilling spectacle. There were pops, cracks, bursts of smoke, flashes, colours and small explosions. When the last package had disappeared into the depths and the fireworks subsided, Spencer and Murray filled the hole with soil. "I wonder what modern day environmentalists would say about that?" muses Murray.

Murray taught about thirty grade three, four, and five students. He enjoyed it immensely. The predominantly Mennonite children were well behaved and enthusiastic. They arrived at school in the forerunners to today's school buses: canvas covered wagons drawn by horses. A step up from closed-in cutters or cabooses, these were bigger, and sported wooden wheels during summer and runners in the winter.

"These wagons had small wood or coal stoves in them to keep the kids from freezing," Murray recalls. "Seemed awfully dangerous to me. But what a quaint sight to see all those covered vans lined up in the schoolyard waiting for the final bell."

One of the van drivers brought Murray's and Spencer's mail from Gem, so they rarely had to go into town. A country store two miles (three km) down the road sold groceries, and each evening they walked a mile (1.6 km) to Royer's dairy farm for fresh milk. Mrs. Royer often gave them fresh baking too.

As winter approached, the men stocked up on canned meats, fruits, and vegetables. In the kitchen they were quite capable. Spencer cooked fine roasts in the oven of the coal stove, and Murray had a flair for cakes, cookies, and pies. Nevertheless, the bachelors were smart enough never to pass up the proffers of a real cook. "Every Tuesday we had a farm lady come and do our housecleaning and laundry and she would make our noon meal. My how we looked forward to those Tuesdays!"

The cook stove was their only source of heat. On cold evenings there was a knack to banking it so it would continue to give heat through the night and still provide embers for rekindling in the morning. Murray and Spencer prided themselves on apparently having acquired this knack. Their pleasure turned sour, however, when one night Murray woke to a house full of thick green smoke. He had to act quickly to alert Spencer and throw open the doors before deadly fumes overcame them. Several weeks later it happened again. Each time they were mysteriously wakened before the noxious fumes put them to sleep forever.

Christmas arrived and school closed for the holidays. Murray and Spencer spent the break with their families in Lethbridge and Medicine Hat. "We couldn't leave anything freezable in the teacherage," Murray recalls. "There was no one to keep stoking the stove for us, so we had to plan carefully not to have too much food left by December 23rd."

Days later when they returned the bitter prairie winter had invaded. Roof studs, floor, furniture, even bedclothes were heavily crusted with frost. They quickly lit the stove and kept the fire roaring all night before the house so much as began to warm. They couldn't even find comfort under the bedclothes without first heating them thoroughly before the fire. It was the most piercing cold they had ever known.

Out of the harshness of winter came spring, and with it sweet scents of new life. One balmy morning, however, the men woke to an uncharacteristically foul smell. Skunk! The pungent aroma lingered all day and was stronger the next. A careful search revealed a hole in the earth embankment around the house. The artful skunk had burrowed in to find a commodious home beneath the floorboards. He wasn't there at the time, so Spencer and Murray plugged the opening with dirt and rocks and considered their problem solved. The skunk, however, had other plans and dug himself back in. Further investigation revealed why. "He" had a nest of babies tucked beneath the teacherage! "The smell got really terrible and we could stand it no longer," Murray recalls. "So on the weekend we tried to smoke the critters out, then left for Calgary, hoping by the time we got back the skunks would have been discouraged and found some other habitat." The strategy worked. When they returned the skunks were gone, never to be seen—or whiffed—again!

The farmers of the Gem district enjoyed good crops due to irrigation, but in the days of lowest ever wheat prices, their toil inevitably met defeat at the hands of the suffering economy. At the end of June, as Murray prepared to move on to another school and Spencer began to contemplate marriage, there wasn't enough money to pay their wages. The best the school board could do was promise to pay them as soon as they were able. Certainly not until fall, when it was fervently hoped the returns of the harvest would be sufficient to cover school taxes. There was nothing for it but to persevere. It was nearly Christmas before the men received the wages owing them.

Spencer stayed on in Gem and Murray went to teach a single grade in Coaldale, Alberta. Out of the midst of the stark depression their year together spawned warm friendship and happy, colourful memories. Gems to last a lifetime!

Travel

. . . .
. . . .

MOST TEACHERS, LIKE almost everyone else, couldn't afford to run automobiles during the years of the Great Depression. Instead they relied on their feet. When feet wouldn't do they depended upon neighbours or the people with whom they boarded for transportation. This might be in the form of saddle horse, horse and buggy, or the famous Bennett Buggy described earlier.

. . . .

"The only school I didn't have to walk to was my first. There one of my pupils and I arrived in a two wheel cart that was hauled by one horse."

Ruth Cowan (nee Hawkins)
Connaught School, Alberta

. . . .

These affairs were sometimes called Anderson Carts, named after Saskatchewan Premier James Anderson (1929 – 1934). In winter, sleighs, cutters, and stoneboats transported travellers over the snow.

With the exception of bitterly cold days, the walk of up to four miles to and from school could be pleasant.

. . . .

"I used to enjoy my walk in the spring and fall. I remember the meadowlarks singing in the trees along the way. I learned to whistle back to them."

Dorothy Howarth (nee Gaetz)

. . . .

"A lot of the land I trekked was virgin prairie. Slight hollows in the prairie filled with water in the spring melt and formed sloughs. In the dry years those sloughs didn't hold their water long. One of my little pleasant experiences while walking to school one spring day was to discover a duck's nest full of eggs on the edge of a slough. Each day from then on I kept an eye on that nest until the little ducklings hatched. One doesn't often get the chance to see nature at such close quarters. I have often wondered where this family of ducks went after the slough dried up."

Murray Robison
Abelein School, Alberta

. . . .

"In the spring I would walk. One lovely morning I was given canned peaches in a cup in my lunch. I told Mrs. Marose that would be fine. It was such a lovely day, I started to daydream. I swung my pail and away it sped.

Everything scattered. I gathered it up and would tell no one. The dog had followed me. It picked up a cookie. No harm done. The dog would eat it. Instead it ran home with the cookie in its mouth. I was caught. When I got home I was asked if I had anything for lunch."

Jeana Stanford (nee Russell)
Montpelier School, Alberta

. . . .

Venturing alone across the barren prairie or through dense woods wasn't always enjoyable. At times a sense of danger and anxiety was an unwelcome companion.

. . . .

"The first year I taught I boarded with an elderly woman and her son on a farm. I walked through two miles [three km] of thick woods on my way to school. Later I found out it was a pasture with some wild animals. I didn't know it at the time, but the owner always followed me home, and back to school."

Evelyn Hardy
Anthony Hill School, Alberta

. . . .

"On my way to school I would have to walk about two miles [three km] up this coulee and then climb the hill to the prairie where the school was, about another two miles. Once in a while when coming home at night I would see the cattle in the valley, and sure enough there

would be the bull as well. There was no way that I was going to go anywhere near that bull. Many was the night it took me a while longer to get home from school."

Murray Robison
Schlatt School, Alberta

. . . .

"The secretary of my school board had a farm near the school. He owned a very mean bull and one day this creature started out to meet me, having got out of the yard. Fortunately the owner caught him before he got very far and I was told he got rid of the animal soon after."

Dorothy Howarth (nee Gaetz)

. . . .

Many boarding places provided the teacher with a horse. Some had never ridden before and had to learn quickly. This mode of travel was sometimes uncomfortable and the occasional difficulty cropped up between horse and rider.

. . . .

"My first home was three and a half miles [5.5 km] from school and I think they saved their spoiled horse for the teacher. One of the horses always shied at a culvert where a coyote had emerged one day. Another one was determined not to stand still until I got on. More than once I was seen leading the horse home. Later on I boarded five

and a half miles [nine km] from school and rode through
dust storms for days. When it started to rain in June I
was soaked morning and night."

Agnes Hunter (nee Burnett)

. . . .

"There was an exceptionally good barn at this school
and it was always full of saddle horses. Pegs on the back
wall were used to hang up the saddles, if used, and bri-
dles. I also rode horseback, my first steed being an old
work horse and very clumsy. One morning she just fell
and rolled on her back with me pinned under her. A lad
riding his Shetland pony jumped off his mount and,
pulling and tugging at my horse's feet, finally rolled her
onto her side and I crawled out. After that I was given
a young, spirited horse to ride and I just loved her."

Camilla Cline (nee Kilborn)
Ribstone Creek School, Alberta

. . . .

"I had at my disposal a buggy drawn by a horse. My first
worry was to be sure the harness was correctly in place on
the horse. Next, be sure the crupper was fastened down
securely. This crupper was a strap attached to the back of
the harness and had to be passed under the horse's tail. I
was frightened to look at the horse's behind because I was
absolutely petrified that the tail may have worked itself
out of this loop."

Stella Ellwood (nee Gardner)
Aspen School, Alberta

. . . .

*"I boarded two and a half miles [four km] from school
and rode horseback each day. No problem there, I was
raised on a horse. The problem was wearing slacks for
riding but having to wear dresses in the classroom.
Sometimes I would just tuck my dress into my slacks
while I was riding and other times I would take a skirt
and change in the little cloakroom at the school.*

*After school I usually stayed a while to prepare for
the next day. When I went to the barn on the first night
I found the stall empty. Polly, the horse I had ridden,
was gone. I didn't know whether some students were
playing a trick on the new teacher or whether Polly had
slipped out of the bridle. A bit embarrassed, I walked the
two and a half miles [four km] home carrying the bridle.
The next night I asked that the last student out please
close the barn door. Sure enough, when I went to go
home, there was Polly standing with her head over the
closed barn door. From then on I took her halter with
me to school and tied her so she couldn't escape."*

Hazel Youngs (nee Ray)
Melvin School, Alberta

. . . .

*"One year there was a heavy wet snow in May. I usually
walked to school but that day I rode my saddle horse. The
trail was narrow and willows and saplings grew along
the edge. The snow had forced these criss cross across the
trail. I had to get off many times to pull them up so the*

horse could get through. I arrived at school very cold and wet. The janitor had built the fire. No children came that day. I dried my clothes and rode the horse home."

Lillian Coulson (nee Thompson)

. . . .

In general, the few who could afford to run cars didn't use them during the winter. They put them up on blocks, drained the water and oil from the engine (or took it out entirely), and removed the tires and battery to keep them from freezing. Even if a car or truck was kept running over the winter, rural roads were often not ploughed, and there was no guarantee they'd be open.

. . . .

"A close friend of my family and a former school teacher was married and living twenty some miles [thirty some km] the other side of Cereal. One cold winter week she arranged for me to spend the weekend with them. Her husband would come for me on Friday and bring me back on Sunday. The weather was cold but nice and the roads were open. It promised to be an exciting time. They lived in a very small house with few conveniences. Their first baby was just a month old. On Sunday we were having such a good time that they persuaded me that I should wait until Monday morning and return directly to my school. That morning the car refused to start. They filled the radiator with hot water since they had no antifreeze or block heaters of course. Though they

cranked it and pulled it with a team of horses—no luck!
Finally in desperation they got a neighbour to take me
back. Well, the students were waiting at school when I
finally arrived about noon."

Hazel Youngs (nee Ray)
Longsdale School, Alberta

. . . .

Travel by horse and sleigh was very common in winter.
Complete with jingle bells, it was the epitome of open-
air travel; fine if the weather was mild, but brutal under
average winter conditions. Straw was scattered in the bottom of the sleigh for insulation and large rocks heated in
the stove were wrapped and used as footrests. Upper
extremities were thickly encased in blankets and robes to
ward off the freezing assault. All but the driver generally
hunched well down into the sleigh box, seeking what little protection they could against the elements. It sounds
harsh, but this form of travel was customary and accepted
without complaint.

. . . .

"One Saturday Mr. and Mrs. Hamm and I set out for
Hythe to do our Christmas shopping. We were bundled
up to our ears with a blanket for our heads and hot rocks
at our feet. It took all day. On the way home the bitter
cold gave way to a warm chinook. Off came the blanket
and we enjoyed the ride home by starlight. The chinook
continued for several days and soon a stream of water

was running down the road. The cold weather returned and the roads turned to ice, making travel hazardous."

Helena Brown
Preston Lake School, Alberta

. . . .

A stoneboat was a large flat sledge used for hauling stones or, when weighted, for dragging over tilled fields to break up clods of earth. When there was much snow on the ground the stoneboat became a unique means of travel.

. . . .

"The roads got blocked with snowdrifts. Nobody could get to town for six weeks. Then I caught a ride on a stoneboat pulled by a horse. Five of us tried to ride on it but we spent most of the time laughing and falling off. It was a six mile [ten km] trip."

Jeana Stanford (nee Russell)
Montpelier School, Alberta

. . . .

The vast majority of rural teachers taught miles away from their families. Many were young, just starting out on life's journey. The initial trip to their new home was often an adventure in itself.

. . . .

"The newly built railway from Shellbrook west ran a mixed train, consisting of several freight cars and one passenger car, in which I travelled to this strange new land. I had spent the night in Prince Albert at the YWCA, arranged by my dad, who was rather worried about his daughter going off into unknown territory. Some of the passengers were rather bothersome, including an elderly gentleman sitting behind me, offering a drink from a bottle, which he periodically presented around the side of my seat. After a slow, tiresome and rather bumpy ride, I arrived at Amiens Siding, where I was met by the trustees of my school."

Mary Cooke (nee Sanderson)
Cresco School, Saskatchewan

. . . .

Teachers did their best to return home for Christmas and Easter. If they lived close enough, they also went home weekends. Some were fortunate to own a secondhand car; others relied on train or bus service.

. . . .

"I bought a 1931 Ford car which I used in summer to travel eleven miles [eighteen km] home for the two days. In winter my dad fixed up a cutter and broke a horse to drive single, so with that outfit I used to drive home on weekends."

Laura Filipenko (nee Ganshert)

. . . .

*"To get to my home in Edmonton I had to travel on [a]
train that [ran] in the middle of the night. I was only able
to go home at Christmas and Easter. I was taken to the
station in early evening and was left there till the train
came along, sitting in a dark little building. I admit that
I was scared to death. Coming back I was dumped off at
5 o'clock in the morning. I only stayed there for one year."*

Ruth Cowan (nee Hawkins)
Connaught School, Alberta

. . . .

*"How to get back to the Hat for weekends was the prob-
lem. The westbound train went through Irvine at 4:00
P.M. Irvine was about twelve miles [nineteen km] from
my school if I sort of 'short cut' over the prairies. My solution was to cut out both recesses on Friday and take only
half an hour at noon for lunch and then let school out at
1:00 or 1:30 to give me time to hike the twelve miles [nine-
teen km] across the prairies to the station at Irvine and
catch the train. I never missed the train once, rain, snow,
or sunshine."*

Murray Robison
Schlatt School, Alberta

. . . .

*"My boarding place was quite close to the highway, mak-
ing it very easy to catch the Greyhound bus to Medicine
Hat. Moreover, it was only about two miles [three km]
to the CPR station at Pashley. The train didn't stop at*

Pashley. To board one you had to flag it down with a
flag by day and a lamp by night. Many were the times
I spent waiting on that station platform with a flag or
lamp in hand peering down the track for the passenger
train to show up."

Murray Robison
Abelein School, Alberta

. . . .

Road conditions any time of year left much to be
desired. With money so scarce, maintenance declined and
in some areas stopped altogether, making travel difficult.

. . . .

"One spring after a cold winter with lots of snow I
wanted to go to my folks' for Easter. The roads were
almost impassable. I finally got into Ponoka by horse-
back. A friend sent two horses and one rider. With
my suitcase tied to the saddle we arrived late and very
tired after a twenty-five mile [forty km] ride."

Mabel Spady (nee Hemeyer)
Park Springs School, Alberta

. . . .

"I remember coming back from a trip home to Calgary.
I got stranded in Rocky. No one came to meet me. Roads
were bad. I had to stay at the hotel overnight and the
next day no one showed up, so a young waitress got the
RCMP to drive me out to within a couple of miles of the

place where I was boarding. The farmer drove me on home. I learned to ride a horse there."

Bertha Brown (nee Vessey)
Chedderville School, Alberta

. . . .

"I met a male teacher from the adjacent district. He had a car, was interested in music, and this was also his first attempt at teaching. On a May 24th holiday we decided to really enjoy the country and drive to an opening lake dance several miles away. Neither one of us knew the way. The roads were not gravelled or marked. There were a few swamps too. We went merrily on our way and had a wonderful time. We were sure we knew the way home. The only right thing we did was to take the right direction. We got on the wrong road and practically sunk. My companion walked some distance to where an older bachelor lived. There was no help given as his one horse had died and the other couldn't be caught. We finally got the car out and arrived home in the early morning."

Mabel Spady (nee Hemeyer)
Park Springs School, Alberta

Louise's Story

· ·
· · · · · · · · ·

LOUISE MCLEAN (NOW Hathaway) had her heart set on becoming a nurse. Her parents, however, had other hopes. In 1934 nurses didn't make much money. Louise was expected to secure a job with at least some financial promise so she would then be able to help pay for the education of her two younger siblings. Besides, Louise's parents couldn't afford a three-year nurse's training course. Instead, they borrowed the one hundred dollar tuition from a close friend and eighteen-year-old Louise was accepted at the Saskatoon Normal School. Ten months later she graduated with a First Class Interim Teaching Certificate.

Next came the daunting task of finding a school. Like all her Normal School colleagues, Louise was forced to compete with hundreds of unemployed teachers for every job opening. It was six months before a telegram from northern Saskatchewan finally gave her the break she needed. The teacher at North Beaver River School near Meadow Lake had resigned. Would Louise be available to replace her? There was no hesitation.

The trip from Streamstown, Alberta, to Meadow Lake took three days. Louise travelled by train, stopping to stay overnight with friends in Lloydminster and North Battleford. She arrived in Meadow Lake at 10:00 P.M. on a cold January night, weary but eager to begin life's newest adventure.

To her surprise, nobody from the North Beaver River school district stood ready to meet her. Instead, the secretary from the adjoining south district waited with horse and sleigh. He introduced himself, then took her to the local cafe for supper, and out to his farm for the night. It was Louise's last glimpse in a long while of civilization as she knew it.

The following day they travelled north along crude trails to the North Beaver River district and Louise caught her first sight of the land where she would live and teach for the next six months.

Without exception, the farmers of the area had recently walked away from established farms in the dust bowl of southern Saskatchewan. Incessant wind, grasshoppers, crop rust, and drought had eaten away their livelihoods. In a desperate bid for a second chance, they had sold or packed all they could, abandoned the rest, and trekked hundreds of miles to the more fertile soil of northern Saskatchewan. Truly pioneers, they cleared the bush, built homes of rough logs, and lived off the land. Hardworking and hospitable, they were civilized people in an uncivilized environment. And they were wretchedly poor.

As soon as Louise arrived they faced a dilemma. A small teacherage was available, but they couldn't possibly allow the young girl to live alone there. She would have to board. But where? Most homes had only two rooms, one of which had a bedroom area partitioned off at the end. It wasn't that nobody wanted to board the teacher, just that no one had room for her. Finally a family of five agreed to take Louise, just until another place could be found. None ever was.

Fortunately, her new family was congenial, for in such cramped quarters privacy was nonexistent. In the tiny back bedroom there were three double beds. The husband and wife shared one, their two sons another, and their seventeen-year-old daughter and Louise, the third. Nothing more than building paper stood between the beds.

The cabin was crude but serviceable, with mud-chinked log walls and planed lumber flooring. A wood-fuelled kitchen range heated the main living area; a smaller stove warmed the bedroom. Washing and drinking water was hauled in and the little house out back served its necessary purpose.

Much to their chagrin, most of the homesteaders relied on government relief. Things like sugar and flour were strictly rationed, but nature didn't hold back its bounty. Men caught jackfish and perch in the Waterhen River and hunted moose, wild fowl and deer. Chickens and a cow provided eggs, milk, butter, poultry, and cream. Cranberries and blueberries were harvested and canned or frozen in great volume. The mother of the house was an excellent cook. Her cranberry and raisin pies particularly delighted Louise, but before she left North Beaver River she became so weary of blueberries she thought she could never eat another one!

Because it was a new settlement, the school was only six months old. Every cost-cutting measure possible had been effected while building it. Logs, and mud to chink them with, were the cheapest and most abundantly available materials. Men who had always made their living on the prairie found them awkward to work with. The result was a school with several gaps in its walls, allowing a view of the sky from indoors. Like Jessie's school in the Silver Fox district, the North Beaver River School made do with a large converted oil barrel for a stove.

Louise had about twenty students. Because there had been no school there previously, age and grade levels didn't match. Some students in their late teens were working at a grade six level. Louise had skipped grade six in her own schooling, putting her at a disadvantage for teaching these young people.

Another disadvantage was no books other than standard readers. Blackboard and chalk were the only teaching tools. Louise spent hours copying work onto the board, erasing it when done, and replacing it with more. Some students finished quickly, leaving her at a loss for where to direct them next. She was torn between admiration and frustration when one conscientious grade two pupil made a point of coming to school early, slipping into his desk, and finishing the entire arithmetic assignment before the school bell rang!

Students and teacher all walked to school. While the others wore jeans and moccasins to keep themselves warm, Louise, unaccustomed to northern winters, had only skirt, cashmere stockings, leather boots, and overshoes for the mile long hike. As a result she developed chilblains. The redness, swelling, itching, and burning in her feet and legs, especially in the evenings, were almost unbearable.

It was impossible to acquire more appropriate clothing. When she accepted the position at North Beaver River School she agreed to a salary of three hundred dollars. Upon arrival, however, she was shocked to learn they could only manage ten dollars a month, and a promise to pay the rest later. Eight dollars paid for room and board. The two dollars left didn't stretch far. Clothing had to be ordered from the Eaton's catalogue. It wasn't until spring that Louise finally managed to get a pair of jeans.

The purchase was timely. With spring came hordes of mosquitoes, blackflies, and sandflies. In those days there were no lotions or sprays to deter the bloodthirsty pests. The best that could be done was to ensure as much skin as possible was covered. Although glad of the jeans, Louise suffered much more cruelly than those who had lived there a while. They seemed relatively immune to the onslaught while the hideous creatures zeroed in on fresh blood.

In an attempt to diminish the pestilence, each night a smudge was carried through the house. Dry grass topped with green in a jam pail was ignited and swung through the air. The smoke created drove out some of the intruders, but not all. Then everyone climbed into bed and the mother spread fine netting over each of them. This warded off mosquitoes and flies. Bedbugs and fleas, however, were another matter. The bedbugs were in the wood of the bedsteads and log walls. Nothing could be done about them. As for the fleas, if you could catch the lively creatures you could kill them, but that was about it.

Encouraging this plague of pests was the spring thaw. As snow melted, water pooled, forming instant sloughs in the many low-lying areas. Travel became dependent upon finding the means to cross them. In the heavily wooded environment, a solution was handy. Loose logs, placed end to end over the water, made shaky makeshift bridges along which people sidled with long walking sticks. The technique required a certain finesse foreign to newcomers from the dry south. Louise's first attempt sent her spinning, quite literally, into the water. It was Easter Sunday and she was dressed in her best for a visit to a neighbour. "Nothing like arriving drenched to the skin!" she smiles.

There were few roads in the newly settled northlands. Those that existed were either ruts or mud, or corduroy roads (like miles of continuous speed bumps). Travel along them took place on foot or by horse. In one way this worked to Louise's advantage. It was customary for the inspector to visit each school in his charge at least once, if not twice a year. Teachers, especially those inexperienced, dreaded his appearance. Good evaluations were vital to ensure a continuing career. The expected call to Louise's school never materialized. Chances were the inspector didn't dare attempt the hazardous travelling conditions. Consequently, she didn't receive her first inspection until after leaving North Beaver River. By then she had gained in both experience and confidence.

As spring wore on things began to dry. One day a mixed blessing fell upon the district. A bush fire. While the homesteaders welcomed the event as a boon to their land clearing efforts, the birds and wildlife were devastated. In terror, animals large and small scrambled desperately to escape the noise, smoke, and flames. Birds were startled and confused, and helpless as their nests tumbled with the trees. For Louise it was a horrifying sight. Afterwards, as she walked the marshy mile (1.6 km) to school, charred trees continued to fall around her, sizzling as they sank into the water of their final resting-place.

Social life thrived in the North Beaver River district. It was what kept the settlers going under circumstances of severe privation. The schoolhouse was the hub of activity. Nearly every Friday night the little building hummed to the sounds of music and dancing. The seventeen-year-old Louise boarded with had become a close and dear friend. Often she and her boyfriend made a foursome with her older brother and Louise to walk to the dances. "A happy memory of such nights," recalls Louise, "was the gorgeous beauty of the Northern Lights which we saw on the way home."

Desks were pushed against the schoolhouse walls to clear a space for dancing (and provide beds for sleeping children). In their excited anticipation, nobody paid attention to which desk went where and whether its belongings went with it. Afterwards, when the men replaced the desks, they were rarely in the right order, and their contents were often scattered. It took a fair bit of time Monday morning to straighten things out. "However, the inconveniences were gladly endured for the sake of the good time," hastens Louise, "because happy times were not numerous."

In the spring an itinerant minister appeared in the area. It was natural for him to conduct church services from the school. Then desks became pews. It wasn't always easy or comfortable for adults to use furniture designed for children (once, when the congregation rose to sing, the "pew" a large lady was sitting in rose with her), but the homesteaders cheerfully persevered. The student minister contributed to the district in other ways too. When Louise organized a field day involving two other schools, he was happy to help.

Single women in the north country were vastly outnumbered by single men, many of whom were seeking a wife. Louise's parents began to feel anxious about the possibility of their daughter marrying and settling down so far from home. At the end of the term they encouraged her to move closer. So serious were they that her father found her a teaching position himself, at Millerdale School, near Kitscoty, Alberta. The fact that teachers in Alberta received higher salaries in general than those in Saskatchewan was simply a bonus.

It was three years before Louise finally received the balance of what the North Beaver River school district owed her. It was also three years before she was able to pay off, with interest, the one hundred dollars her parents had borrowed to put her through teacher's training at Normal School.

She has no regrets: "In spite of the hardships, the cold, learning to balance on a wet log, there were so many compensations. It was six months I would not have missed for anything. To compensate were seeing the beauty of pink ladyslippers, the surprise at the height of a sandhill crane and the awe of watching the colourful ever-changing Northern Lights. There was too the very deep admiration for those homesteaders who had the courage and the will to leave cultivated farms and comfortable homes in southern Saskatchewan to begin again to build a life in the virgin-forested land of the north. They were in truth—heroes!"

The School (I)

. . . .
. . . .

To SAY THAT rural schools during the Great Depression were ill equipped is an understatement. If they existed at all, budgets for supplies and replacement of outdated material were completely inadequate. In many cases, even the buildings left much to be desired. Cracks in the walls and ill-fitting doors and windows made them draughty, allowing dust and snow to filter in. Roofs leaked. Stoves, the only source of heat, were unpredictable and sometimes makeshift. The teacher's desk might be nothing more than a homemade table.

. . . .

"As with most buildings at that time the school lacked insulation and was hard to heat. A crack in the wall by the library let in the daylight showing where, at some time, cloakrooms had been added to enlarge classroom space. The old pot-bellied stove had most of its jacket removed but was still woefully inefficient."

Hazel Youngs (nee Ray)
Melvin School, Alberta

. . . .

*"We never did get any books, so we got lessons ready
using whatever could be found in the small library."*

Anne Westgard (nee Benell)
Weetslade School, Saskatchewan

. . . .

*"The few library books were well worn, the big dictionary
in a sad state of disrepair, the few roller maps so brittle
that when one was pulled down it cracked in another
place and usually a piece fell out. The big clock on the
wall behind my desk hadn't kept time for years, but the
rope on the big bell in the belfry was in good condition,
as was the bell. On clear cold mornings that bell could be
heard for miles. The blackboards were large and in good
condition, but the chalk was scarce and the erasers well
worn. We were allowed no coloured chalk to make fancy
decorations on the blackboard for special occasions."*

Camilla Cline (nee Kilborn)
Ribstone Creek School, Alberta

. . . .

*"A blackboard at the front and a smaller one on the east
side, with chalk supplied by me, were the only teaching
tools. A map case on the east wall held three pre-1918
maps, which could be rolled down to cover assignments,
spelling lists, et cetera. There was no lighting, not even a
kerosene lamp. On dark days we gathered around the*

stove, door open to give enough light for me to read to the children. For concerts and card parties the parents brought their own Aladdin lamps."

Hazel McKenzie (nee Watson)
Ridgeway School, Alberta

. . . .

Lack of instructional material, particularly books, was a major problem. School libraries were unrecognizable by today's standards. Some consisted of only four or five ragged books. Teachers supplemented what little they had in whatever way they could.

. . . .

"We used all the material available. We begged and borrowed. My parents had saved all the old school textbooks we had used in our school years and these provided a wealth of information. I also begged from a friend an old set of the Books of Knowledge *and a set of six encyclopedias. Those I kept at home for material to make lessons more enjoyable. I insisted that these borrowed books be used with caution, and it was amazing how much they were used and how well they were handled. There were no copiers so all the material had to be hand written. I used the blackboard and every night it filled to capacity with work for the next day or a map to be left until the study of it was completed. I did have a large map of Alberta, which I had made in Camrose, that hung on the wall and was used daily by one class or another.*

*You can be sure Talbot, Coronation, and Ribstone Creek
School were marked on that map."*

Camilla Cline (nee Kilborn)
Ribstone Creek School, Alberta

. . . .

*"There were no reference books at my first school. Just
chalk, a broom, a ball, and a bat. I even hesitated to give
the pupils a list of necessary books as money seemed
almost nonexistent. We did get two large boxes of old
books from Ontario. They were mainly old Ontario readers and books no longer used, so of little use for reference.
The Eaton's catalogue was used extensively for posters
and various other purposes."*

Agnes Hunter (nee Burnett)

. . . .

*"Mr. Owen Williams, the inspector from Lethbridge,
was especially helpful, dropping in to bring a pile of
magazines such as the* National Geographic *for our
small library cupboard."*

Hazel McKenzie (nee Watson)
Ridgeway School, Alberta

. . . .

"The library was very limited. I remember adding to it from my salary. Any special decoration or teaching aids were supplied by me. Supplies were very limited, although this school rated higher than many."

Ruth Powell (nee Caldwell)
Alice Hill School, Alberta

. . . .

"When I knew my salary would be paid I didn't mind buying some crepe paper and ribbon for Christmas decorations, or a big box of coloured chalk. Every month we had a new decoration on the blackboard and the little children spent hours colouring it. Oh the joy from one precious box of coloured chalk!"

Camilla Cline (nee Kilborn)
Rough Meadow School, Alberta

. . . .

Few schools were lucky enough to house a piano or an organ. Those that did often couldn't afford to maintain it. Creaky, out of tune instruments were still used and appreciated for music classes and Christmas concerts.

. . . .

"Here we had an old reed organ. The bellows leaked air. Some stops were missing, others didn't work, and some keys were silent. But we used it anyway for our daily singing. A talented musician, a lady, came to help with the annual Christmas concerts and she could really get

the music out of that organ! Revival church services were
often held in the school and she could make the organ
heard above the lusty singing of 'When the Roll is Called
Up Yonder.' She was a joy to have as she could play with-
out the sheet music. Hum the tune and she could play it."

Camilla Cline (nee Kilborn)
Rough Meadow School, Alberta

. . . .

Despite having limited instructional materials, rural
teachers taught many subjects to many students at many
different grade levels. In the forty minutes scheduled for
one subject, he or she would have to teach eight or more
lessons, depending upon the number of grades in the
school. This was difficult, especially for those teachers just
starting out.

. . . .

"In Normal School we were taught all the school subjects
by professors, and they certainly were efficient. But one
thing was forgotten: how to make out a timetable that
would allow for perhaps a two minute lesson and an
assignment of seatwork to keep that grade busy for the
entire period. Our practice lessons gave us at least forty
minutes and we had a week or two to prepare seatwork.
Mr. Frame, my first inspector, taught me how to teach two-
or three-minute lessons and assign the follow-up work.
My first timetable was a very complicated piece of work."

Camilla Cline (nee Kilborn)
Ribstone Creek School, Alberta

. . . .

"Being a city girl, never having attended an ungraded school [all grades in one room] I worked harder than any time before or since. I tried to teach each grade separately, religiously following the course of studies for each grade and subject, from grade one to nine. A few beginners couldn't speak English and needed special care. The older pupils were all boys, nearly as old as I. But they were well behaved and helpful and I enjoyed the time spent with them. I soon learned to combine grades and subjects and let them help each other."

Hazel McKenzie (nee Watson)
Ridgeway School, Alberta

. . . .

As the experiences of Hazel, Murray, and Jessie have illustrated, language barriers were common. Many of the farmers at that time were new Canadians. They sent their children to school to learn and be educated in English. Often their children, in turn, taught them. Occasionally a rural teacher offered English lessons to adults on his or her own time.

. . . .

"This was a community in which there were many Ukrainian and Polish people, so language differences caused some difficulty. The beginners knew no English, some of the others very little, and English was my only

*language. However, with the help of a grade eight girl
we were able to communicate, and it was surprising how
quickly they learned."*

Muriel Lugg (nee Smith)
Fidelity School, Alberta

. . . .

*"There were thirty-six names on the register such as
Oskoboiny, Sudnik, Tolway and Dashevsky. There was
one British family named Light with whom I boarded.
The others were Ukrainian, Polish, Jewish, Mennonite,
or German. I taught all the grades from one to eight.
They were talented, responsive youngsters and I
enjoyed them."*

Helena Brown
Preston Lake School, Alberta

. . . .

Lack of worldly experience was also an impediment
to learning. Born and raised on the farm, children rarely
ventured farther. Family vacations were unheard of.
Travel to the nearest town for groceries and mail was an
infrequent outing; books, newspapers, and magazines
were scarce. Access to the outside world was limited in
every way.

. . . .

"The parents would go to town on Saturdays to get supplies. They never took their children. Miss McKiligan, the preceding teacher, took the children to town to let them see a store, a post office, a town."

Jeana Stanford (nee Russell)
Montpelier School, Alberta

. . . .

"The Longsdale School had a very small enrollment, only eight to thirteen students from three or four families. Their experiences were very limited. None had ever seen a passenger train. Two passenger trains a day did pass through Cereal, seven miles [eleven km] south, but both passed in the middle of the night."

Hazel Youngs (nee Ray)
Longsdale School, Alberta

. . . .

"The pupils at a very isolated school heard an airplane flying over the school and we all went out to watch. I'll never forget the look of amazement on their faces as they saw their first airplane."

Agnes Hunter (nee Burnett)

. . . .

"To have books to read aloud to the class I brought my own. Since I had grown up in a different social climate, we talked a great deal about where I had been."

Dorothea Laing (nee Dove)
Wardlow School, Alberta

. . . .

"Resource teaching material was nonexistent. Teaching history and geography was difficult. They looked at me almost in disbelief when I told them that from my home I could look west and see the Rocky Mountains. How could they grasp the vastness of the world or the meaning of a map?

There was an outside door to the basement, a lift up board affair, which lay flush with the ground with steps descending beneath it. This door was never used but it made a great base for outdoor games. A board in this door had become loose and although the school board knew of it nothing was done until Mamie, one of the older girls, fell through and broke her collarbone. This meant a trip to the Calgary hospital, about 150 miles [240 km] away. Mamie saw great wonders—passenger trains, streetcars, electricity, plumbing—a taste of the outside world."

Hazel Youngs (nee Ray)
Longsdale School, Alberta

. . . .

With no other staff on the premises, and the nearest school four to eight miles [six to thirteen km] away, the teacher, often only nineteen or twenty years old, faced every conceivable situation alone, struggling to cope as best he or she could.

. . . .

"Rural teachers had to depend on their own resources, taking full charge of everything. There was no principal to turn to, no secretary or aide to help, or even any other teacher close enough with whom to discuss problems."

Hazel McKenzie (nee Watson)
Ridgeway School, Alberta

. . . .

"A one room school, ten grades, and eleven pupils. Imagine how little I knew about teaching, how incapable—the gopher tails, frozen egg sandwiches for lunch, arriving at the school, forty below zero, to find the stove wouldn't work for Andrew, so had to light it. Every day, petrified of the school inspector's visit."

Olga Allison (nee Burch)
Wealthy School, Alberta

. . . .

"Shortly before 9:00 one morning, the children came rushing into the school to tell me that one of the horses had been cut in the barbed wire fence. I told two of the boys to bring her up to the door, as I was just ready to pass out a departmental exam to my two grade ten students. How in the world could I take care of both situations? Well, I had the two students move their desks to the door where I could see them while they worked. Then I grabbed a piece of rope that the globe had been hanging on, in preparation for applying a tourniquet to the horse's bleeding leg. I passed out the exam, started

*the students at the dot of 9:00, and hoped the other stu-
dents would manage without me. Next I turned to the
task of taking care of the horse. I sent an older boy at
once to phone Mr. Hindmarsh, the owner of the horse.
Fortunately, Dot was quiet, so I proceeded to apply the
tourniquet to her hind leg. Dot shook her leg a few times,
liberally spattering my nice voile dress with blood. I
remembered to loosen the tourniquet after a short time,
but she had lost a lot of blood. Luckily the owner arrived
soon afterwards, loaded her and took her to the veteri-
narian, who said that I had probably saved her life. Was
I a proud girl! The story has a happy ending. Dot recovered completely and presented the family with a foal the
next year. The two grade ten students passed all their
exams, including the one they wrote the day I played
vet! What did it matter that I taught the remainder of
the day in a blood-spattered dress?"*

Muriel Lugg (nee Smith)
Fidelity School, Alberta

. . . .

*"One winter day there was a terrible blizzard. Telephone
lines were down. I was dismissing the children at noon to
head for home. John, one of my grade six pupils who had
not come to school that day, arrived at the door crying.
His mother had died; he was alone at home. So I went
home with him. I had told one of the students to tell his
father to come. John and I waited and waited. I can still
remember it so vividly. I had never seen a dead person,
but began to think I could not let her stiffen, propped in*

bed as she was. John brought out some clothes. We ironed them, then dressed and laid out the corpse."

Olga Allison (nee Burch)
Wealthy School, Alberta

. . . .

"During morning recess the long row of stovepipes collapsed. Fortunately, no one was hurt. There were a couple of smouldering sticks in the old jacketed heater, so there was a small amount of smoke. The caretaker lived a few yards behind the school, so I sent for him to come to help. However, he was noted for imbiding too freely over the weekends, and since this was Monday morning, he was still slightly inebriated. He was certainly in no condition to be at the school, but he got the stepladder, valiantly tried to ascend, but was having great difficulty. I finally persuaded him to let one of the older boys try his luck, which he did, and the pupil succeeded in putting the stovepipes up again.

But this was not the end of the story. Dear old Mr. Nesbett fished the smoldering sticks of wood out of the heater, carried them carefully outside, and proceeded to empty our cream can of water on them. 'To put out the fire,' he said. This meant we had no drinking water for the rest of the day. (The pump wasn't working!)

At any rate, I went back into the school, and had no sooner got the class settled down when the door opened a few inches, a head appeared, and Mr. Nesbett called, 'Goodbye Miss Smith.' I said goodbye, and the door closed. Amid some smiles and giggles, we settled down once more. But the door opened again, and again we heard, 'Goodbye Miss Smith.' I said goodbye and thanked him again. But nothing daunted, he tried again. 'Goodbye Miss Smith.' This time I said very firmly, 'Mr. Nesbett, you must leave now, because we have work to do. Goodbye!' and he left."

Muriel Lugg (nee Smith)
Fidelity School, Alberta

. . . .

"One day a beginner, a little girl, didn't return to class at 1:00 P.M. Someone had seen her going to the girls' toilet but no one remembered seeing her after. Well, she wasn't there, so the first search was in the grove of trees just across the fence from the toilet. We called and walked but no sign of her. I thought perhaps she had gone home as those trees were on her path home so I asked a bigger boy to go on my horse and see if she was there. While he was gone our little girl came from those trees. She had fallen asleep and hadn't heard us. Her frightened parents and neighbours arrived to help search but were relieved that she was back at school. She wasn't upset. She was just playing and got tired so sat down and fell asleep. Guess that is the innocence of childhood."

Camilla Cline (nee Kilborn)
Rough Meadow School, Alberta

. . . .

"One day a skunk got under the school and stayed for three days while the school, the teacher, pupils and lunches were saturated with that burnt skunk smell for days."

Agnes Hunter (nee Burnett)

. . . .

"One winter a nest of skunks holed up under the school. They apparently got in through a small hole in the foundation. About March they started to stir around and the odour would get very strong in the classroom. We set a trap and in the course of time we got thirteen. Later we had one in the boys' toilet. The secretary of the school board used carbon monoxide on that one."

Camilla Cline (nee Kilborn)
Rough Meadow School, Alberta

. . . .

"A bright star appeared on the horizon. The Halloween dance in the town of Whitla. Annie's parents would take us and bring us back home [to the teacherage]. A night of dancing and laughter and at midnight a sumptuous supper of coffee, sandwiches and cake. We bid Annie's parents goodnight and thank you at our door. We didn't invite them in as it was late. A big surprise awaited us. Some pranksters had paid us a visit. They, like everyone else, had a skeleton key. Our bed and mattress was thrown over on the floor, the bedding scattered, sugar, among other things, thrown around. We set to and put things straight, and then off to bed in the wee small

*hours. I'd had enough of frustration, and much as I loved
my pupils and teaching, I would leave. I didn't report the
break-in. I was afraid of retaliation and besides, the cul-
prits were unknown except for bits of gossip."*

Ruby Hughes (nee Scott)
Golden Sheaf School, Alberta

. . . .

*"Halloween time seemed like prank time. It was an
evening to overturn outdoor toilets. To have school
function toilets had to be up. Some board members came
to dig a new pit. As they were digging the pit they came
across a gopher wrapped in a grass bed. My boys brought
the gopher indoors and placed it by the furnace. We
watched it yawn but it never awoke out of the hiberna-
tion stage. I truly expected to see it run around the
classroom, but it didn't. Eventually the boys took it out
and buried it."*

Annie Tym (nee Sankey)
Jewett School, Alberta

. . . .

*"We had some interesting wildlife, both indoors and out.
Mice used to run along the top of the blackboards and
bats paid us a visit on occasion. One day when I was
doing some work before going home I had left the door
open. I heard a pitter-patter of little feet and a small animal came right up to the front and stood in a corner and
gnashed his teeth. I had no idea what it was. I remember*

I jumped up and stood on my chair and wondered what to do. I threw a few things at him but that was doing nothing to scare him. So I crept to the back to get the broom and managed to get him out. Later I found out it was a groundhog. I had never seen one before.

Then one morning when I was dusting the desks as one of my janitor chores, I looked down and saw the biggest garter snake I had ever seen. I speedily retired to the outdoors to wait for some of the older boys to arrive. They got it out but were not too happy with it either, even if it was a harmless garter snake."

Ruth Cowan (nee Hawkins)

. . . .

Few things instilled more fear in a rural teacher than the prospect of the school inspector's visit. He (in those days it was always a man), came around at least once a year to evaluate the teacher, students, condition of the school, and school board records. A teacher's career hinged upon his reports. The difference between a good and bad report was often the difference between a permanent teaching certificate and having one's license revoked. Teachers seldom knew when the inspector would appear and lived in terror of it. Many coached their students as to how to behave when he arrived and designed special lesson plans for his visit. The inspector's intentions, of course, were only to be helpful, but the power he held was awesome.

. . . .

"The inspector wrote full reports, with carbon copies for the department, the local school board, and the teacher. It was important for the teacher to have two really good reports, and to write a book test, before receiving a permanent certificate. We never knew when the inspector would pop in. Our district kept changing inspectorates and in my three years there we had three different inspectors, from Fort Macleod, Vulcan, and Lethbridge."

Hazel McKenzie (nee Watson)
Ridgeway School, Alberta

. . . .

"The seventh day of school Inspector Aylesworth paid us a visit. Pretty scary! Now I realize his aim was to assist new teachers, but then...!"

Hazel Youngs (nee Ray)
Longsdale School, Alberta

. . . .

"I remember one inspector's visit. He took a class to the board and gave them a certain question in mensuration to solve [finding areas and perimeters]. 'What is the first thing you would do?' he asked one lad. The boy tried to explain that he would multiply this by that and then...et cetera. 'What is the first thing you would do?' the inspector kept sternly repeating. The boy was scared. He thought he was doing it right. Finally the inspector handed him the chalk and told him to go to the board and do it. Thank goodness! He went to the board and drew a diagram, and I began to breathe again."

Hazel Youngs (nee Ray)
Melvin School, Alberta

. . . .

*"How will I ever forget one school inspector who arrived
at noon hour when we were out playing ball. The children
thought he was a real good sport when he joined in the
ball game. After the usual two hours of inspection he
came back into the classroom and accused the boys of
putting scratches on his new car. I asked them if they
had done it and when they denied it I believed them. The
inspector was furious. He said I had neglected to teach
them to respect other people's property and his parting words were: 'You just might lose your certificate!'
Needless to say I was upset that afternoon. However I
did hear later that when the inspector had visited in the
district that morning the trustee's turkeys had perched
on the car and scratched it, so I didn't worry anymore
about losing my certificate."*

Agnes Hunter (nee Burnett)

. . . .

*"Our school yard was not fit for a ball diamond because
of the cacti, so a farmer consented to let us use a piece
of his pasture adjoining our yard for a playground.
Every day, in the wind and dust, we spent our noon hour
playing ball. Every one of us, big and small. On one particularly windy, dusty November day we were deeply
involved in our game. It was nearly 1:00 P.M. and not one
of us noticed a car wending its way down the hill from
the west. Nor did we notice that it came into the school
yard. The first I saw was a well dressed, strange man*

talking to one of the big girls. He was asking, 'Which one is the teacher?' This man was the school inspector, Mr. Frame, a friendly, well-respected man. What a mess we were in that day, windblown and dusty. The school board and I smiled at the comment on his report: 'I am always pleased to see a well worn ball diamond and the teacher out playing with the children.'"

Camilla Cline (nee Kilborn)
Ribstone Creek School, Alberta

Dorothy's Story

. . . .
. . . .

DOROTHY BENTLEY STRUGGLED to get through school. When it was finally over, she was dismayed to learn her father expected her to become a teacher. In his wisdom he believed teachers could find work eventually, even during the bleak depression. Dorothy wouldn't dream of defying her father, so in 1937/38 she dutifully attended Normal School in her hometown Calgary and with a first class teaching certificate set out to find a job.

She applied for every available position, half hoping she'd hear nothing. By the end of September, with not a solitary offer made, she began to think she was off the hook. Then a call from Cadogan caught her off guard. A resignation in the Silver Lake School north of that town had created a sudden opening. The job was Dorothy's if she wanted it. "Where is Cadogan?" gasped the astonished girl. She rushed to a large map of Alberta mounted in the stairwell of her home. Extraordinarily detailed, it indicated the tiny village way up in east central Alberta. Half way around the world!

Scared to death, Dorothy packed her things and boarded the train that would carry her away from city and family for the first time in her life. Eighteen long hours later, the sight that met her eyes as the train pulled into Cadogan was less than inspiring: a lengthy string of outdoor privies. Long a thing of the past in cities, they symbolized her complete departure from the comfort and convenience of home. A farmer's son met Dorothy at the station with horse and buggy. Recognizing her innocence he took it upon himself to offer some sage advice: "The first day you go to school you take out the strap, lay it on the desk, and keep it in good sight or you'll have trouble!" Dorothy was too unnerved to decide whether he was joking or serious.

As they pulled into the farmyard where she was to board her apprehension grew. Men everywhere! It was only a visiting threshing crew but their numbers overwhelmed her. And flies! Hordes of them! She was shown a room above the farmhouse kitchen. The only heat it received eased up from the kitchen through a grate in the floor. It was one of the warmest rooms in the house, but Dorothy, accustomed to central heating, found it dreadfully cold.

The following day Dorothy crossed the pasture with her farm family to attend Sunday service at the United Church. As soon as they arrived she was accosted by a well-meaning but alarmingly commanding woman. "You must be the new school teacher! Would you like to read the scripture today?"

Dorothy had never read scripture aloud to anyone, let alone a room full of strangers. Shy and frightened, she blurted out a blunt, "*no!*" Instantly she was horrified at having sounded so rude. The stunned countenance before her confirmed it. Even the people Dorothy was with were shocked. "Nobody has ever turned Mrs. S— down before! We just never say no to her!" Ever afterward Dorothy har-

boured the uncomfortable suspicion she had been rele-
gated to Mrs. S—'s bad books. When she discovered Mrs.
S—'s son was a student in the school, her uneasiness grew.
It wasn't a pleasant beginning to a teaching career.

The following day, gripped with fear, Dorothy stood
before fourteen strange young faces. Aside from a brief
episode of practice teaching in Normal School she had
never experienced nine grades in one room. Additionally,
the presence of several large boys caused her concern.
She recalled the words of the farmer's son, but didn't take
out the strap as advised. Fortunately, time proved her
fears unfounded. She was delighted to find the children
well behaved and responsive. The older children were even
too conscientious. They spent so much time telling their
younger siblings to toe the line that Dorothy frequently
had to remind them that they had their own work to do.

The lack of teaching aids was frustrating. The library
had only a dictionary, an atlas, and a few storybooks. Some
of Dorothy's students were particularly keen for knowledge. On trips to Edmonton she bought every appropriate
book she could find for them. After her first year she purchased two sets of encyclopedias on a time plan with her
own money. She was supposed to receive yearly inserts to
update them, but none ever came.

Dorothy's greatest difficulty was teaching French as
the grade nine option. She had taken it in school and
could read and write a little of the language, but couldn't
speak it properly. Ever resourceful, she wrote to other
teachers for help. They obligingly sent information and
somehow Dorothy muddled through. She knew, however,
that that was no way to teach, so when the inspector came
she explained her predicament. He suggested art and music

for the grade nine option instead. Dorothy was elated, as she was already teaching art and music to the entire school. The following summer she took a typing course so she could teach typing as an option too.

Classroom activity soon settled into a comfortable routine. But trouble lay ahead. The terrifying Mrs. S— was about to enter Dorothy's life once more. Mrs. S—'s son was exceptionally bright. He had a remarkable imagination and a gift for spinning fantastic tales. Unfortunately, he also had cerebral palsy. His attempts at making himself understood were severely frustrated, and his movements were awkward and hard to control. Dorothy, however, saw only his talent. She was excited about his potential and encouraged him to pursue it. She was even beginning to understand his unique way of communicating. Then disaster struck.

Despite his handicap, the children treated Mrs. S—'s son as they would any other and one day he found himself in a schoolyard scrap. Dorothy rushed to intervene, but just as she launched herself into the fray Master S— let fly a stunning blow that hit Dorothy squarely in the eye. The black and blue shiner she sustained couldn't possibly be hidden. She tried hard to defend the boy, even stating her injury came from walking into a door, but the other students weren't so tactful. Mrs. S— soon learned the whole story. She was mortified, and wasted no time in withdrawing her son from school. Dorothy felt thoroughly dejected and would have done anything to have him back. But Mrs. S— was adamant. She would teach her son by correspondence at home. Dorothy, already intimidated by her earlier episode with the woman, couldn't bring herself to beg.

Although Dorothy felt isolated living so far from the

city she soon lost the homesickness she initially suffered. The Silver Lake people were friendly and sociable. Dorothy played piano for the church; dances, weddings, and picnics were common. Every Saturday night farm families gathered in the streets of Provost, the nearest market town, to shop and visit.

It wasn't long before the young teacher had herself a beau: the older brother of one of her students. It became a delicate matter to separate personal life from school life. One day after school Dorothy's boyfriend, Bud, appeared on his horse outside the open classroom window. "Get on!" he urged.

"Not on your life!" replied Dorothy. She was leery of horses, and for that matter, any animal with a mind of its own. Besides, the student janitors were still at the school and Dorothy didn't want to appear improper. As it turned out, she had no choice in the matter. Suddenly she found herself airborne as Bud's younger brother picked her up and hoisted her, skirts and all, straight through the window and onto the back of the horse. So much for propriety!

Despite being nervous around horses, Dorothy knew that living in the country, she should know how to ride. One day at Bud's farm she tried to ride a horse that wouldn't budge. Wanting only to be helpful, Bud's brother Bill gave the horse's rump a good hard slap. The startled animal jumped and bolted straight for the barn. Dorothy managed to duck just before it raced through the low barn door. Not soon enough for Bud's horrified mother, though. Certain that Dorothy's head would be smashed against the barn wall, she promptly fainted. Unfortunately for Bill, she revived quickly. He received a sound walloping, screams of "You could have killed her!" reverberating in his ear.

Although Dorothy didn't flaunt it, neither did she think it necessary to keep her romance a secret. The school children knew about it. One of them even wrote 'The teacher loves Bud' in the back of his textbook. It was an innocent prank, but trustees checking the condition of the books came upon it and were incensed. The teacher was expected to be of the highest moral character. It wouldn't do for children to be talking about her love life. Dorothy received a stern admonishment. In turn she kept the offending student after school to erase the words and he got into trouble at home for being late. A hard lesson learned for both student and teacher.

In the city Dorothy travelled by streetcar. Now, with the exception of Saturday night trips to Provost, she walked everywhere. It was only a quarter mile (half a km) across the pasture to school but going farther afield was more difficult. When her father bought a new car and made her a gift of his old one, she was grateful. She soon learned, however, that driving in the country bore little resemblance to city driving. It was fine when the weather was dry, but the car wouldn't maneuver in prairie mud and under such conditions Dorothy usually landed up in the ditch. Once she ended up in a tangle of roots, and in winter the car couldn't be used at all.

A solution to these problems was at hand. As was so often the case with farmers who couldn't survive on the devastated prairies of the thirties, friends of Dorothy's decided to head for British Columbia. They convinced Dorothy to "sell" them her car for the trip and agreed to send payment back as soon as they found work. She never heard from them again.

Dorothy's contract was for seven hundred dollars; more

than many rural teachers made. It wasn't long, however, before she too discovered that the school board couldn't pay. The first money she saw was at Christmas when they drummed up enough for her to return home for the holiday. In the meantime she had to run a line of credit for room and board and other necessities. Early in the New Year, the Provost School Division formed and Dorothy's school became part of it. From then on she collected a regular paycheck and eventually managed to pay off all her bills.

Despite her initial reluctance Dorothy was an effective educator. Her own earlier difficulties gave her compassion and understanding. She had a talent for presenting concepts in different ways until every child could grasp them. Her students did well.

Dorothy came to love and appreciate the people of the Silver Lake district. Although she and Bud went their separate ways, and Dorothy eventually left the school for another, she never wandered far from the area. She married George Murray and settled down near Provost to raise a family of her own. Sixty years later, she lives there still.

The School (II)

IT WASN'T LONG before the effects of the depression became evident in rural school children. Clothing became progressively worn and ragged. Malnutrition was epidemic. Some children defied the odds by remaining robust in spite of it, but others withered to pale shadows and were prone to illness. Margaret Hill (nee Cottrell) who taught at Nestor School, Alberta, in the late thirties, recalls shoeless children coming to school with feet wrapped in gunny sacks. For some of them, survival depended upon turnips. What children brought to school in their lunches often reflected conditions at home.

. . . .

"The lunch pails were filled with plain food: bread, pancakes, or biscuits with some kind of a spread. Most people milked a few cows so skimmed milk was readily available. If there was nothing for the lunch pails then the children brought a kettle of homemade soup and it was heated on the top of the old Waterbury heater. Potato or vegetable soup was the most common. They did lack

fresh fruit, but most families had canned rhubarb and saskatoons."

Camilla Cline (nee Kilborn)
Rough Meadow School, Alberta

. . . .

"One family brought lunches of bread spread with lard. I remember having difficulty enjoying my own lunch pail."

Ruth Powell (nee Caldwell)
Alice Hill School, Alberta

. . . .

"One family in this district was very poor. Often the boys came to school in winter without underwear. Occasionally they did not bring lunch because there was no flour at home to make bread and they were too proud to bring vegetables in their lunch pails."

Lillian Coulson (nee Thompson)

. . . .

Teachers who boarded in the homes of the district suffered along with the children.

. . . .

"For six weeks I was given peanut butter sandwiches. I used to open my lunch pail and throw them into the stove when no one was looking. I like peanut butter but not every day."

Jeana Stanford (nee Russell)
Montpelier School, Alberta

. . . .

Teachers were in a unique position to witness the needs of the children around them. More than once they attempted to ease the privation of their students.

. . . .

"1930 was the beginning of the depression and sometimes I would invite the school to my house to have dinner. Then I would get mostly fruit and the foods I knew they were not getting at home."

Dorothea Laing (nee Dove)
Wardlow School, Alberta

. . . .

"When it was cold I would make tomato soup for the children. Parents took turns sending milk. I supplied the cans of tomatoes, soda, salt, et cetera."

Jeana Stanford (nee Russell)
Montpelier School, Alberta

. . . .

People were poor, but they still maintained a good deal of pride. Sometimes the perfectly innocent good intentions of the teacher backfired, with disastrous results.

. . . .

"I was concerned about the poverty in some of these families. I had heard that Eaton's and Simpson's mail order people sometimes donated parcels for the poor. I wrote, stating the need, and was rewarded with a parcel of remnants from each one. I contacted a lady who was a good seamstress and she made several pairs of pants and shirts for boys. Thinking only of helping I gave some clothing to two boys who were in rags. Immediately these garments were returned to me by their father. He was very angry and informed me that he would look after his children without help from nosy outsiders. The clothing was given to another family who accepted it gratefully. The teacher was taught a lesson and I learned to be more sensitive to people's feelings."

Mary Cooke (nee Sanderson)
Cresco School, Saskatchewan

. . . .

With the ravages of inadequate diet and clothing taking their toll, it's surprising sickness wasn't more of a problem. Few families could afford a doctor. Summoning one wasn't even considered for such "trivial" diseases as measles, mumps, chicken pox, and so on. When children met with mishaps or came to school sick, the teacher acted as nurse, taking the role in stride along with his or her many others.

. . . .

"The school did not have any type of phone, so a sick child had to stay in school all day, spreading colds, measles, chicken pox, or whatever."

Hazel McKenzie (nee Watson)
Ridgeway School, Alberta

. . . .

"One big drawback was the school yard, which was polluted with cacti. Very beautiful when in bloom but not good for the barefooted students. In summer there were many cacti spines to be removed from hands and feet. My only instrument was a very sharp needle. No iodine or bandaids. When one was unfortunate and got cut we used a handkerchief to stop the bleeding. A handkerchief dipped in cold water was used to stop a bleeding nose, or to ease the ache from a bruise.

One day twin girls were coming to school riding double when the horse shied, throwing them off. One girl was kicked as she fell. They came on to school but the one who had been kicked was dazed and in shock. What to do about her? She couldn't ride the horse home and wasn't able to be at school. I asked an older boy to take my horse and ride to a farm about a mile [1.6 km] away. The folks there had a coupe car. They came and took the girl to her home where she was bedridden for several days."

Camilla Cline (nee Kilborn)
Ribstone Creek School, Alberta

. . . .

*"One family sent their three boys to school with impetigo.
One other boy contracted it. However, the doctor sent
out a brown salve for them to use with instructions for
keeping bedding and clothes clean. Thankfully it didn't
go through the school. Later we had a real epidemic of
whooping cough. I got a bottle of Ipecac for that. When
a pupil started to cough, out came my teaspoon and he
got his dose. That usually caused vomiting to remove the
phlegm from the throat. Fortunately it was spring, so
they ran outside for that operation. Children's illnesses
were not worrisome to the parents, unless one became
very ill. All the so-called childhood diseases were just a
matter of course."*

Camilla Cline (nee Kilborn)
Rough Meadow School, Alberta

. . . .

*"Early in the autumn of my second year at Abelein
there was a polio [infantile paralysis] epidemic. It was
bad enough to close all schools in the country—I'm not
sure about the city—for a week. Then, when we opened
after the week of closure, a school nurse came out to
the schools, one day a week, for a month to inspect the
children—and teacher—and spray our throats."*

Murray Robison
Abelein School, Alberta

. . . .

"One of the children had ringworm. He came from a very very poor home. Most of them did. Even though they were poor they were clean, but this family wasn't clean. He got ringworm. I kept the patches bandaged and covered up because he wasn't getting any treatment at home. I learned afterwards that I should have sent him home. In the end I did. He eventually came back but he had scars."

Mary Cooke (nee Sanderson)
Cresco School, Saskatchewan

. . . .

"The first time I encountered body lice was when a neighbour knocked on the school door. He advised me that some of the class had body lice. What a shock! I hadn't ever seen one. I asked my class if any were aware of this. One small girl offered me a sample. I, as the teacher, had to visit this home and offer advice. It is the hardest errand that I have ever done."

Mabel Spady (nee Hemeyer)
Park Springs School, Alberta

. . . .

"We had a session of head lice in the school that was a frightening experience for me. The child's hair was combed with a fine tooth comb over a newspaper placed on a school desk. Any sign of these crawly creatures and the boy or girl was sent home with a note to the parents."

Stella Ellwood (nee Gardner)
Aspen School, Alberta

. . . .

*"After holidays I returned for another term. Two weeks
later I came down with the mumps. Everyone in the district
caught this painful disease. School was closed and harvest
was beginning. Those mothers! I never heard of anyone
going to the doctor twenty-five miles [forty km] away."*

Mabel Spady (nee Hemeyer)
Park Springs School, Alberta

. . . .

*"We placed cans of water on top of the stove to provide
proper humidity. This probably prevented many colds but
on frigid mornings the walls and blackboard were covered with frost. I often swept up a dustpan full of frost
from the wainscoting and it was towards noon before the
blackboards were dry enough to use."*

Hazel Youngs (nee Ray)
Melvin School, Alberta

. . . .

*"Colds, flu, and diseases spread rapidly through the school.
The children were in close contact with one another. They
all stayed for lunch over the noon hour and sat in double
desks. The drinking and washing facilities comprised
of a pail and basin. The towel was hung by the basin and
all the children used it. Many did drink from a common
dipper."*

Mabel Spady (nee Hemeyer)
Park Springs School, Alberta

. . . .

The potential for the spread of disease was greatly enhanced by the water conditions at the school. A well was at risk for all manner of contaminants, from bugs to drowned animals. This didn't seem to bother the children in the least. When a new well was dug at Mooresville School in Alberta, a dead mouse in the very first pail of water drawn didn't fluster Margaret Hill's (nee Cottrell) students. They casually threw it out, drew another pail, and drank happily from the well from then on. Water arrangements inside the school weren't much better.

. . . .

"At school a drinking dipper was supplied, but I had each family bring a cup to drink from, which I washed at the end of each school day."

Ruby Hughes (nee Scott)
Golden Sheaf School, Alberta

. . . .

"I might have mentioned the open water pail and communal drinking dipper. How did we ever survive all those germs? Even if a child brought her own drinking cup, her friends borrowed it."

Hazel Youngs (nee Ray)
Longsdale School, Alberta

. . . .

The single wash basin and towel were a haven for germs. The basin might be rinsed with leftover drinking water at the end of the day, while the towel received an infrequent laundering. Some schools didn't have a towel.

. . . .

"We had no paper towels or tissue of any sort. If we washed our hands we dried them either on our clothes or by blowing on them. This method, I am sure, was the forerunner to our modern blowdryers."

Camilla Cline (nee Kilborn)
Ribstone Creek School, Alberta

. . . .

Whether it was walking, riding horseback, or skimming along on wheels or runners, most travel was open air, so weather was a constant concern. Some schools ran a March to November year, avoiding the winter months. The majority of schools, however, functioned September through June. The janitor (in many cases the teacher) was responsible for arriving early to light the fire and warm the building before students appeared. In winter, this was a bitterly cold task, and just one of the many discomforts suffered throughout those frigid months.

. . . .

"I walked one and a half miles to school [2.5 km], had to do the janitor work, and start the fire after I arrived. It was quite often forty or fifty [minus forty to minus forty-five degrees Celsius] below zero."

Madeline Bailey (nee Chapman)
Gillion School, Alberta

. . . .

"The gas barrel heater was fuelled by wood. I remember how cold it was starting that schoolhouse fire each morning. No heat was available overnight as wood was used for fuel. The pupils rode horseback or walked. Many did not have proper clothing, shoes, et cetera, for the extreme winter cold."

Mabel Spady (nee Hemeyer)
Park Springs School, Alberta

. . . .

"A big pot-bellied stove stood part way toward the back of the room with a long stovepipe extending to the front of the room, which helped to keep the room warm. Five nights a week the stove was banked with coal to keep the heat on and the room warm for next morning classes. Monday morning, cold but bright, I returned to school early enough to build a fire in the school's old pot belly when I noticed that one of the stove's legs had come loose. Thank goodness it happened during the weekend, otherwise it would have been banked for the night. I awaited the arrival of each pupil and promptly sent them back home. No school today! I sent word to the school trustees.

*The stove was promptly repaired and we started school
the next day."*

Ruby Hughes (nee Scott)
Golden Sheaf School, Alberta

. . . .

*"My school had a big round furnace towards the back of
the room to keep us warm but in sixty below [minus fifty-
one degrees Celsius] weather we were far from warm. The
kids rode horseback to school and in cold weather I had
only half my pupils. I didn't teach. All we did was huddle
around the stove."*

Evelyn Hardy
Anthony Hill School, Alberta

. . . .

*"Women did not wear pantsuits then, so heavy skirts,
high top overshoes, scarves, and mitts bundled us. Often
the drifts would be deep enough to cover the overshoes,
filling them with snow. Then we would sit around the
hot stove, feet on the nickel ring, wet clothes steaming.
I suffered from painful chilblains.*

*Of course, all the lunches in lard pails would be frozen
solid. They would be put on the stovetop, then the sandwiches taken out and toasted, or often scorched, filling the
room with smoke."*

Hazel McKenzie (nee Watson)
Ridgeway School, Alberta

. . . .

"The school had a small pot-bellied heater in the centre of the classroom which gave out good heat to those fortunate enough to sit near it. In the winter we didn't use the entry, but the lunch pails, overshoes, mitts, and all outer wearing apparel were kept on the floor around the stove."

Camilla Cline (nee Kilborn)
Ribstone Creek School, Alberta

. . . .

Blizzards were not uncommon. The first signs of an approaching storm struck fear into a country teacher's heart. Most of the children had long distances to travel. In a rural setting, familiar landmarks were crucial for a sense of direction. Blowing snow wiped them out instantly, and the dangers of getting lost were serious. Dismissing the class early enough to beat the storm home was a race against time not always won.

. . . .

"During the lunch hour my attention was drawn to the ominous clouds forming in the northwest. By 1:00 P.M. I was quite frightened for it looked like a bad blizzard would soon strike. The class bundled up in their jackets and overshoes, and cautioning them to hurry home and to stay together I sent them on their way. Many walked across the fields, but if they arrived home before the storm they had a good path to follow. Luckily it was close to two hours before the wind came up and the first few flakes began to fall. That storm was a three-day blizzard

and a cold one too. When we went back to school, after the storm, the row of desks next to the north windows, and the floor, were all dusted with a heavy coat of snow. And, oh, that school was cold!"

Camilla Cline (nee Kilborn)
Rough Meadow School, Alberta

. . . .

"We had a bad blizzard blow up one winter afternoon. Sending the children home at four was out of the question so we sat tight, hoping the storm would soon subside. However, it was several hours later before it did, and then the parents came in sleighs to pick up the children."

Jessie Pendergast (nee Erskine)
Hillmartin School, Alberta

. . . .

"One day a very bad storm came up suddenly. A blizzard so blinding that it was unsafe to send the children home. Parents who lived fairly close came for their children. The rest of us waited out the howling winds by playing games, reading stories by firelight, and eating any left-over lunches until the storm abated and parents were able to get through."

Hazel McKenzie (nee Watson)
Ridgeway School, Alberta

. . . .

"In December a howling blizzard came up and one of the fathers who lived close to the school took the pupils to their house. This was only a three-room house with a family of five, however we were all glad to be inside. After supper, as one of the boys was separating the milk, he moved the lamp over by the window and in a short time there was a banging at the door. Two men and a boy came in. They were covered with snow and their faces and hands were frozen. The four-year-old boy was badly frozen. We rubbed his body and moved his arms and finally he began to cry. Their car had become stuck in a snowdrift and they had been following a fence when they saw the light at the window. There were twelve people there that night and only two beds so we played cards all night. As we sat there the water dripped off their frozen faces and ears. There were very few phones in the district, so there were anxious parents that night."

Agnes Hunter (nee Burnett)

. . . .

Blizzards often forced closure of schools for days at a time. No one knew who would be returning to school and when. It was up to the teacher to ensure that someone was there when students arrived back from their unexpected hiatus.

. . . .

"There was a blizzard that raged for three days. Men tied rope from the house to the barn so they would not get

lost. On the fourth day I walked nearly a mile [1.6 km] to school. Just one family came. They had a horse and sleigh. I got them warmed up and sent them home. When Saturday came all came to school with sleds. The snow had drifted to the roof of the building. What fun we had going to the roof and sliding down. We marked it as a school day too!"

Jeana Stanford (nee Russell)
Sherburne School, Alberta

. . . .

White blizzards in winter gave way to black blizzards the rest of the year. These were dust storms so abrasive that blowing soil and sand stripped paint from buildings and decimated crops. Nothing escaped the onslaught; dust even made its way between the pages of closed books.

. . . .

"It's hard to describe the intensity of those dust storms in the thirties. On the level prairie you could see the huge black dust storm rolling towards you, then suddenly all would be dark as the dust blotted out the rays of the sun. You couldn't even see your hand in front of you. It was impossible to keep the dust out of the houses and by the time the storm had gone through, it would be on everything, making for a real job of cleaning."

Murray Robison
Abelein School, Alberta

. . . .

Other pestilences during the thirties included grasshoppers, army worms, and tent caterpillars. In great numbers they swelled slowly across the land, leaving destruction in their wake.

. . . .

"This was the year of army worms and dust storms. In their march the army worms invaded the school, came through the screens and under the door and then crawled on. One time we had planned a friendly ball game with a neighbouring school, and after both teams had arrived a dust storm came up. We couldn't see to play ball and it was some time before we could start out for home."

Agnes Hunter (nee Burnett)

. . . .

"Another frightening time was a black blizzard. Huge black clouds of soil from the north, gathering dust as it swept over, caused a complete blackout. Precious soil from the fields drifted against the tumbleweed-covered fences and into the houses and school before moving on. This was followed by a plague of tent caterpillars eating everything in sight. Masses of them climbing any obstacle, moving forward in a steady stream."

Hazel McKenzie (nee Watson)
Ridgeway School, Alberta

Eileen's Story

FOR SIXTY DOLLARS a month Eileen Barkley rose from a lumpy teacherage bed at 6:00 A.M., scampered to the one-room school next door, chopped wood from the pile of tree trunks outside, cleaned out the stove inside, built a new fire, dusted the school, replenished the water supply, taught classes all day, supervised recesses and noon hour, swept the floor, and planned the following day's lessons for thirty-two students in ten grades.

She had just completed Camrose Normal School, class of 1934, and was glad to have a job. Having graduated with only three homemade dresses to her name she spent the last of her savings on a few clothes and a large supply of pork and beans before moving to the teacherage next to her central Alberta school. It was the first time Eileen had ever lived alone. "I was frightened after dark," she recalls, "until I got up the courage to investigate the nocturnal noises and found [they were] made by cattle settling down by the teacherage for the night."

Eileen soon met challenges in the classroom as well. She quickly realized a girl left in grade six by the former teacher was really only functioning at a grade three level. To complicate matters, her parents were friendly with school board members, who therefore consented to promote her to grade seven. When Eileen approached the trustees about it she met stiff resistance. The previous teacher, they informed her, had given the girl high marks. Furthermore, in order to prevent future misunderstandings, Eileen was instructed to administer exams to every child in every grade in every subject once a month. This was an extra hardship on an already overburdened schedule, but Eileen gracefully complied. Each month she rode horseback behind the chairman's child to his home to present her results. The entire evening was devoted to meticulous scrutiny and intensive questioning. By the end of it, Eileen wanted to tear her hair out, but sheer fatigue prevailed and she collapsed instead onto her host's spare bed. After spending the night, she was deposited back at the school by 6:00 A.M., in time to attend to her chores.

Another harrowing event was the school inspector's visit. He always appeared promptly at 8:00 A.M,. an hour before school began. After examining the school register, daily plan book, and students' work, he sat silently at the back of the class, observing both Eileen and the children. Occasionally he joined in. One dreadful day he called to the blackboard the girl who had been wrongly promoted and gave her a grade seven math problem. She was completely stymied!

Cold weather saved the day. While the girl stood helpless at the board, the inspector slipped out to warm up his car. Eileen quickly told her exactly what to do. When the inspector returned, the problem was solved. There were no questions asked!

The children of the depression were bounty hunters. The government paid a premium for the body parts of pests they most wanted to eradicate. Where Eileen lived it was gophers. In the spring the prospect of a penny a tail made gopher snaring the favoured noon hour activity, especially among the boys.

"One lad objected to giving up [his] pursuit when the bell rang," Eileen recalls. "I was promptly visited by the father who thought I should allow his little boy to wait until he caught that last gopher. I explained that if this was allowed, the others would expect the same, and as a result there would be no school in the afternoons. The father found it difficult to understand why this exemption could not apply only to his son."

A similar bounty was attached to magpies. Eileen had the dubious honour of holding the parts. "Gopher tails and magpie legs were getting more than a bit high by the time I was able to turn them in."

Eileen enjoyed her school in the country but after three years decided to resign. It was a risky decision with jobs so scarce, but she had a plan. She knew that as an experienced teacher it would be easier for her to find work than it would be for her sister, just finishing Normal School. She also knew that if she left her current position chances were good her sister would be hired to replace her. The plan worked. Not only was her sister hired, but Eileen also secured another position without delay.

Her next school was some distance away and once again she lived in a teacherage. When her brother drove her out to the place and saw the tar paper shack he was horrified. He begged Eileen to return home with him. She refused. She was used to living alone now and accepted the conditions of privation. "There was a cookstove . . . heater . . . small cupboard, a few pots and pans . . . chipped dishes, four chairs, a table and a coal oil lamp in the main room," Eileen relates. "In the other was a bed with a soiled lumpy mattress and filthy blankets. In lieu of a clothes closet there was a shelf from which hung a curtain. Once again I had provided my own bedding." The cookstove and heater had little effect in the uninsulated building. In winter, with both fully stoked and blazing, water in the tea kettle froze on the back of the stove.

Happily, the lack of charm and comfort in this humble dwelling were compensated for by the cheerful warmth of the people in the area. Eileen was invited everywhere, and usually returned home laden with meat and produce. On Saturdays, neighbours took her along when they travelled the eight miles (thirteen km) to town. If they went during the week they gladly ran errands for her, bringing back mail and groceries. "The teacherage was a weekend meeting place for young people, both married and single," she fondly remembers. "We played games, had skating parties, and went to dances. In that school district I made many lifetime friends."

Once again, Eileen taught about twenty-five pupils from grades one to ten. Like their parents, they were friendly and cooperative. Her only problem was that of so many teachers of her time: not enough money to pay her. She had to wait until school taxes were due, then hope enough was collected to cover her wage.

Early in 1938 Eileen's school was incorporated into a division including several schools and by Christmas she was transferred to one of them. She was told she was needed to reinstate order after a disastrous term served by a young girl from the city who was unfamiliar with country ways. In exchange, Eileen was offered her choice of available schools the following September. She made it clear she would be exercising this option.

Life was difficult at the interim school. "I didn't enjoy boarding," Eileen says. "Although my hosts were kind in their own way, I didn't wish to invade their privacy, so I spent most of my time in my room." An old horse carried her to and from school each day. The going got rough when spring run-off washed out bridges along the way. Despite the hardships Eileen performed well. At the end of June a delegation approached her. "They asked if I would stay if they fixed up the school attic as living quarters with a ladder up the wall for access. When I asked who would carry up water, coal, and wood and take down ashes and slop, they realized their request was futile."

By September of 1939 the Great Depression was at long last grinding to a halt. With the luxury of choice before her, Eileen selected a well-equipped school complete with attractive teacherage. Two years later she became Eileen Toliver, and under ever improving conditions continued to influence the hearts and minds of young scholars for many years to come.

The School (III)

· ·
· · · · · · · ·

How to handle discipline problems in the one-room classroom wasn't addressed in Normal School. Normalites were on their own in that department. How they fared had little to do with age, size, or gender and seemed more to pertain to personality, or perhaps sheer luck, than anything else. The diminutive, young, inexperienced schoolmistress might be able to maintain perfect order while the older, more experienced and portly schoolmaster with the booming voice may not. Children seemed able to quickly size up any teacher and arrange their behaviour accordingly.

Managing discipline problems weighed most heavily upon new teachers, often not much older than their oldest students and perhaps smaller in stature. Indeed, to the outsider, many of these teachers were indistinguishable from their pupils.

· · · · · · · ·

"One day a young man stopped at the school and when I answered the knock on the door he asked to speak to the teacher. I said, 'I am the teacher.' His mouth dropped

open and he was speechless for a few seconds. This only goes to show how young I was!"

Muriel Lugg (nee Smith)
Fidelity School, Alberta

. . . .

Although the strap was the most common and frequently used form of discipline, many teachers objected to it and either rejected it entirely, or used it only under extreme circumstances. In time each teacher developed his or her own methods for keeping children in line.

. . . .

"This school was a real challenge to discipline. Imagine facing one girl and six boys taller than myself! Their previous year [had been] very lax in discipline as well as in their lessons. The teacher seemed content swirling in his easy chair smoking his pipe. The school board informed me that they desired a change. The first day I confronted all the students with requirements. They were not permitted to pop out of their seats like jackrabbits to see who was passing by on the road. We organized softball teams and I was out with them every recess and noon hour. I wanted them to know that I was interested in their activities. I was the umpire of every game. Students returned to practice for an hour after supper. This activity discontinued after the snow came, but was back in greater force early in the spring. In early June we had a competitive softball league Sports Day, playing with four other neighbouring schools. The first spring my pupils won two

*shields and the second spring four shields. We truly
became famous. No more discipline problems of any kind.
I won the children's hearts."*

Annie Tym (nee Sankey)
Jewett School, Alberta

. . . .

*"When someone warranted it I would turn them over my
knee and spat them with my hand. It didn't hurt them,
but oh the embarrassment! One weekend I stayed at my
boarding house. I remained in my room. I heard voices so
I listened. The children were telling a cousin what I did if
they were naughty. One voice said, 'No teacher could do
that to me.' I quickly opened the door and went out. I
flipped that boy over my knee and gave him a spat. The
Hudson children were elated. The cousin turned out to be
fourteen years old. I couldn't have done it if it had not
been a surprise."*

Jeana Stanford (nee Russell)
Sherburne School, Alberta

. . . .

*"I rang the bell after the noon break. Only the little chil-
dren came in and sat down in their desks. I rang it again.
Finally they were all in and seated. They claimed that
they did not hear the bell, which I knew was not true. I
cautioned them that if it ever happened again I would be
at the door with the strap. Some weeks later they tried
this stunt again. True to my word I stood by the door
with the strap. Everyone late got one swat on the hand.*

That ended the rebellion. Last summer one of these former students visited me. She said she was the instigator of that trick. They knew they were in for it so she volunteered to go first and the bigger ones next in hopes that I would be played out before I got to the smaller children. I weighed only a hundred pounds. We both had a good laugh over it."

Lillian Coulson (nee Thompson)

. . . .

In the vast majority of rural schools discipline problems were negligible to nonexistent. Children harboured the utmost respect for the teacher's authority and knew that any disciplinary action taken at school was bound to result in consequences at home as well. Some teachers had the ability to win the children's hearts completely. This benefited both students and teacher alike, as the children were content and worked hard to please. There was nothing they wouldn't do for their cherished mentor.

. . . .

"I never took anything to drink in my lunch kit, just had a glass of water at school. There was such a rush every day to bring my water at noon that we had to arrange the children's names alphabetically on the board so that they could take turns.

There were always wild strawberries in the outer areas of the school yard during the summer. The children would pick them at noon, sometimes half a jam pail full, and insist that I take them home for our supper.

*One day two of the pupils insisted that their mother
had invited Ella and me for supper the next night.
Therefore, after I finished my work the following day, we
set out for the children's home. We arrived about 5:00 P.M.
and found them already eating supper. No one asked us
to join them so we visited for a while and then left. We
were scarcely out of earshot when Ella collapsed in the
bottom of the buggy convulsed with laughter. When we
arrived home a very surprised lady [Ella's mother] hurried to get us some supper. We found out that it had been
wishful thinking on the part of the two children, and we
had not been invited at all."*

Muriel Lugg (nee Smith)
Fidelity School, Alberta

. . . .

*"In 1934 Enterprise Education was introduced into the
schools. It really meant teaching all subjects, or at least
as many as possible, around a single theme. For my grade
five student, Harry, I decided to 'Take a Trip to Europe.'
This meant preparations for the trip, travelling across
Canada by train, crossing the ocean in an ocean liner, et
cetera. We were doing famously; Harry really seemed to
be in the spirit of the activity. So much so that he really
thought we were going to go, for real. It was his sister,
Esther that put me wise. Poor Harry. It was such a disappointment when he found out it was only a fantasy."*

Murray Robison
Schlatt School, Alberta

. . . .

*"What a most rewarding moment I experienced at Aspen!
Because of an unavoidable breakdown of my '27 Ford
coupe I arrived a good fifteen minutes late at school. I
found the children all in their places, books open, two of
the older girls helping the grades one, two, and three, and
all busy doing their daily assignments."*

Stella Ellwood (nee Gardner)
Aspen School, Alberta

. . . .

*"I boarded about forty rods [about two hundred m] from
the school at the home of the secretary-treasurer. They
had two children attending, which posed no school problems. I went home for dinner at noon. At first I was a bit
leery about leaving the classes unsupervised, but was
told, 'That's what they always did.' Luckily no problems
arose from this."*

Hazel Youngs (nee Ray)
Longsdale School, Alberta

. . . .

The children had fifteen-minute recesses both morning and afternoon, and a one-hour lunch break, so there
was ample time to release their energy in play. Unless the
weather was completely inclement they played outside.
There was no playground equipment, so imagination
became their greatest resource. Snow forts and secret hide-
outs inspired fantasy worlds. Many traditional and invented
games required few, if any, props. Common were Kick the
Can, Red Light Green Light, Hide and Seek, Duck on a

Rock, and Tag. If there was a slough nearby, the children skated or played ice hockey in winter, using sawed off branches for sticks and a rock or a road apple (animal dropping) for a puck. Those who didn't own skates played in whatever footwear they had. The teacher often joined in, sometimes as player, sometimes referee.

When too miserable outside there was plenty to do inside. The blackboard was a favourite medium for amusement. Hang the Man, Tic-Tac-Toe, X's and O's or just drawing pictures were great pastimes. Indoor games included Blind Man's Bluff, Jacob and Rachel, Hide the Thimble, and others. Some teachers introduced students to Checkers, and organized lengthy tournaments involving all the grades.

One activity was favoured by far over all the others: baseball. On dusty, makeshift diamonds in every rural schoolyard a game was always at hand. Every child, regardless of age, gender, or ability was invited to participate. Provided the ground was bare and dry enough they, and most often Teacher as well, could be found deeply immersed in the sport.

. . . .

"One day, while I was playing first base in the ball game, a grade nine boy hit the ball, ran for first, and knocked me down. Everyone was shocked, including Devon, but when I got up laughing they all relaxed. Devon always says that I fell for him before I fell for my husband!"

Muriel Lugg (nee Smith)
Chailey School, Alberta

. . . .

Despite the absence of materials and play equipment, teachers never had a problem with bored or idle children.

. . . .

"If the snow was deep enough some of the boys came to school on homemade skis, pulled by a horse. After lunch all of us would take turns ski-joring behind the patient horses. If it was too cold we played games indoors, or had a square dance to the tune of a mouth organ. In summer, baseball was the favourite, although a form of cricket when there were not enough players for baseball was fun. Games like Red Light, Pom-pom Pullaway, Anti-I-Over [over the top of the school], involved all ages."

Hazel McKenzie (nee Watson)
Ridgeway School, Alberta

. . . .

"The board did not supply any playground equipment. In winter the children played games out in the snow: Prisoner's Base, Run Sheep Run, Fox and Geese, et cetera. In summer they played softball. They gave a few cents each and bought a softball, bat, and catcher's mitt. We also had a basketball court out on the grass. A former teacher had built a backstop and hoops, which were put up on high posts."

Lillian Coulson (nee Thompson)

. . . .

"Ball games with neighbouring schools were great fun.
A good-natured parent would load the children into a
big truck and transport them several miles. This created
good fellowship and good sportsmanship."

Muriel Lugg (nee Smith)
Chailey School, Alberta

. . . .

A few teachers had music or theatrical training, which
they gladly incorporated into the school program. In some
areas this developed into the opportunity to participate
in regional festivals.

. . . .

"During my years at Melvin the rural Music-Drama
Festival was started. It was held at Olds and included
schools from Cremona and Sundre in the west to Two
Hills in the east. It was a huge undertaking and we all
learned a lot. Our school won the first one—we had done
a lot of work in that field—and we captured the shield
once more before I married in 1938."

Hazel Youngs (nee Ray)
Melvin School, Alberta

. . . .

"A rural music festival was held in one of the larger
schools. Did the pupils and I ever work! We learned
poems, songs, plays, choruses, et cetera. Every child par-
ticipated. Parents helped. I think nearly all knew most
of the parts. Sherburne had never won. The day came.
Everyone arrived. I stood at the back of the school. I
recited every poem, sang every song, repeated every line
in the play just moving my lips so the participant could
see me. The last item was the school chorus. I led it and
then went out the door and threw up. I was sick. I went
home and went to bed for two days. We were the top
school. The people were elated! So was I!"

Jeana Stanford (nee Russell)
Sherburne School, Alberta

. . . .

The highlight of the year in any rural school was the
annual Christmas Concert. While it was most exciting for
youngsters, it also gave parents and members of the district
a much appreciated evening out and the opportunity to see
for themselves the work of the teacher and students.
Teachers were expected to take a no-holds-barred approach
to the event and had to dig deep into their bag of tricks to
pull it off. It was no small feat for the many who had never
been trained in dramatics, music, or stagecraft. In the eyes
of the district, how well they fared was often the yardstick
by which their value as a teacher was measured. This was
perhaps never truer than during the years of the depression
when both material and financial resources were slim.

Each Christmas Concert was expected to include a vari-
ety of recitations, marching drills, skits, choruses, dances,

rhythm bands, monologues, dialogues, plays, solos, duets, quartets, and numerous other forms of entertainment. The creative powers of the teacher were taxed to the extreme. Costumes, props, and scenery were fabricated from crepe paper, brown wrapping paper, old clothes, curtains, bedspreads, sheets, tablecloths, cheesecloth, flour and sugar sacks, packing cases, old lumber, and bits of flora from the surrounding countryside. Rhythm band instruments were such things as wooden blocks covered with sandpaper, wooden spindles from old furniture, empty containers filled with dried lentils, hollow cylinders stretched over with sturdy fabric, and jingle bells from harness.

A makeshift stage of planks and sawhorses was erected and a tree brought in. The students enthusiastically decorated these and the entire schoolroom with homemade trimmings. Many teachers dipped into their own pockets to buy materials for decorations, costumes, scenery, and props.

. . . .

*"I really put my all into producing that first concert.
I don't recall much of the program but I do know that
I went to town trying to stage it. I had made a backdrop
by cutting out a stained glass window frame on strips
of brown paper glued together and pasting coloured bits
of tissue paper over the cut out portions. Once this was
hung I could illuminate it with coal oil lamps from
behind. The effect was quite stunning, or so the locals
thought. Never had they seen a concert with such back-
ground scenery and such costuming."*

Murray Robison
Abelein School, Alberta

. . . .

"The one big event in those days was the school Christmas Concert. Some of my pupils were quite talented and we put on a Christmas Concert that the community really complimented me on. We had a lot of fun preparing it, too. We usually started the first week in December and spent quite a few school hours, which suited my pupils very well."

Laura Filipenko (nee Ganshert)

. . . .

"I'm sure we wasted two months preparing for the Christmas Concert. What an event! I can still remember the excitement. The school secretary arriving with the tree, everyone making the decorations and decorating it, the lavish costumes, the hours of practicing."

Olga Allison (nee Burch)
Wealthy School, Alberta

. . . .

"Mothers and teacher would spend many evenings making angel costumes, animal faces, and hunting up Grandma's clothes which were stored away somewhere in a trunk."

Stella Ellwood (nee Gardner)
Aspen School, Alberta

. . . .

After the concert Santa came to visit, passing out gifts and treat bags to every child present. It was usually up to the teacher to arrange for an appropriate Santa and there was much conjecture over who it might be. Then the stage was dismantled along with the seating for the audience (benches made by placing planks over desks). Desks were pushed against the walls to clear a dancing floor, lunch was served, and the gala evening continued.

. . . .

"The Christmas parties were the event of the year. Every school had one. The poems, plays, songs, et cetera were work but fun. Of course Santa came with gifts for everyone. I had a friend come from a district west of Taber. No one could guess who it was. I never did tell them. Then the dance, lunch, and so on. Children were put to bed on desks pushed to the walls."

Jeana Stanford (nee Russell)
Montpelier School, Alberta

. . . .

During the depression Santa's visit posed a problem. Most school boards couldn't afford the makings for the treat bags, let alone the extravagant expense of a gift for each child. Fund raising efforts were only minimally successful, as people were themselves in want. Although ideally it also included candies and nuts, it wasn't unheard of for a treat bag during the depression to consist only of an apple or perhaps a Japanese orange.

The T. Eaton Mail Order Company was a godsend when it came to the gifts. Normally, money was raised in the district and an order placed to the catalogue for a gift for each child. Often the mail order firm was simply sent the lump sum of money along with the number, ages, and gender of the children. The firm selected a gift for each youngster, then wrapped and shipped it back. During the depression years, however, the amount that could be spent on each child dwindled dramatically and was often inadequate for any gift, regardless of how small. Nevertheless, Eaton's came through with unheard of generosity. They frequently sent items that far exceeded the value of the money remitted, and in some cases even donated gifts. No child was left empty-handed and all were delighted with the prized "store bought" presents.

. . . .

"In late November preparations began for the Christmas Concert. I had heard that the teacher's worth was judged by the annual Christmas Concert, so excitement mounted as that date drew near. I was also instructed to write to Eaton's for donations towards Christmas gifts for the pupils. So in December a parcel arrived with a gift valued at $2 for each pupil and even one for the teacher. These were wrapped so it was a complete surprise for everyone. There was also a quantity of hard candies which we made up in bags with popcorn balls."

Agnes Hunter (nee Burnett)

. . . .

The annual Christmas Concerts were so popular that people from the surrounding districts often attended each others', scheduling their own so that no two would fall on the same night. This had the added advantage of giving teachers the rare chance to visit colleagues and compare their work with that of other schools.

. . . .

"For entertainment the Christmas Concert was the big event. Every child had a part in songs, plays, drills, recitations. About every four miles [six km] there was a little school and as everyone wanted to go to all the concerts, the teachers had to arrange dates to avoid conflict."

Hazel McKenzie (nee Watson)
Ridgeway School, Alberta

. . . .

Of course no Christmas Concert ever came off without a hitch. Lines were forgotten, children failed to appear on cue (or appeared when they shouldn't), costumes fell apart or tripped up their occupants. Children peered from behind the bedsheet stage curtains and chattered a little too loudly in the wings. Although it invariably mortified the teacher, all this was taken in stride by the audience and considered merely part of the merriment.

. . . .

"The annual Christmas Concert was the big event of the school year. We spent a good month practicing for it and every pupil from grade one to nine had a part in it. Of course the proud parents turned out in full force for the final evening event, and treats were given out to all the children. I heaved a great sigh of relief when it was over, even if some performers forgot a few words of their recitations or sang a little off key."

Dorothy Howarth (nee Gaetz)

. . . .

"At one of our concerts we were presenting the Nativity Pageant. Mary was sitting holding the baby Jesus and the choir was singing 'Star of the East,' when suddenly one of the older girls fainted. She fell right on top of Mary. No light load! Imagine the consternation of Mary, the singers, the teacher, and the audience! However, the girl recovered quickly, rejoined the singers, Mary got over the shock, and the program continued."

Muriel Lugg (nee Smith)
Fidelity School, Alberta

. . . .

"I really think that many times a teacher's ability was measured by the quality of those concerts. One program I shall never forget was at Melvin. That winter both measles and chicken pox were rampant and many students were stricken in that final week before the big event. Their places in the program were eagerly filled by others who were of course familiar with the parts. But

*on the very night of the concert, after an after school cup
of hot soup, I myself broke out profusely with the chicken
pox. The students rose to the occasion and put the concert on alone. I still treasure the letter of commendation
I received from the district for that. The worst part of it
was missing all the holiday parties and festivities."*

Hazel Youngs (nee Ray)
Melvin School, Alberta

. . . .

*"One Christmas Concert Eve I was really hurt when one
of my favourite families failed to attend. At the close of
the small concert I was handed a note to 'please go to this
family's home.' I couldn't imagine why! When I arrived
I was shown a new baby! Mother and Baby were doing
well. No fuss. No doctor or nurse. No special attention.
Another daily occurrence."*

Mabel Spady (nee Hemeyer)
Park Springs School, Alberta

Ewen's Story

. . . .
. . . .

EWEN NICHOLSON WAS one of the lucky ones. The school inspector lived in his hometown—Wadena, Saskatchewan. Immediately after Ewen graduated from Saskatoon Normal School, Mr. Henwood helped him find a job. On 30 June 1934, Ewen found himself on his way to Partridge Hill, a district in the isolated bush country of east central Saskatchewan. As he bumped along in the car beside his father, who would be dropping him off in a new life just as surely as a new home, Ewen wondered about the adventure before him. Little did the eighteen-year-old realize that it would represent the most challenging six months of his life thus far.

Located south of Hudson Bay, Partridge Hill, like Louise's North Beaver River area, was populated primarily by destitute grain farmers driven from the choking dust bowl of southern Saskatchewan. Ewen found the school secluded in the bush. In one corner of its single room stood a four foot by eight foot [one metre by two metre] partition: Ewen's living quarters. No door, just an opening in the wall. Ewen peered into the shadows of the little compartment. It was empty, completely bare. No bed, no cookstove, nothing. With a sigh he carried in his few belongings and proceeded to do what he could to settle in. Sleep eluded him that first night. Never before having lived outside of town, he felt utterly alone in the unknown wilderness. The blackness and strange night noises pressed in upon him. "I was scared out of my mind," he admits. He had been told that an exconvict passed by the school earlier. His qualms were spiked by a terror that the man would return. The biting cold gripped him as relentlessly as the fear. He had brought along three blankets and layered them on the floor to cushion himself from the rough planks, but they provided little comfort. His efforts at sleep were useless. He sat quivering in the school all night, his twenty-two-calibre rifle clutched in his arms.

The next day Ewen determined to improve his lot. The excon had not returned and he felt safer, but something had to be done about his sleeping situation. Gazing thoughtfully about, he hit upon a solution. The area surrounding the school was rife with tall grass, never before cut by human hands. Ewen gathered it up by the armload, carried it into his cubbyhole, and arranged it in piles on the floor. These he covered with the blankets. Well pleased with the results, he turned in that night with a smile of satisfaction.

His pleasure was short-lived. Sometime after retiring, the gradual awareness of a distinctly uncomfortable sensation tugged Ewen from sleep. As he regained consciousness he realized his legs were itching savagely. He groped in the dark for his flashlight and immediately directed its beam beneath the blankets. To his horror, the light caught hundreds of tiny creatures bristling in frenzied motion. Fleas! Ewen leaped from his makeshift bed and wasted no time disposing of the infested grass. Thereafter he went back to sleeping on the cold hard floor. Anything was better than fleas! It was several months before the school board finally found him a bed.

Ewen soon came to know the settlers in the area. They were good people, but he quickly realized that education wasn't their top priority. Mere survival was. Having lost everything in southern Saskatchewan, they were struggling to begin again with nothing. Abundant trees provided them with wood for homes and fuel, but were a curse when it came to scratching a living from the land. Stumps, roots and brush had to be wrenched from the soil before it could be tilled and planted, and there were no guarantees that the cleared land would be fruitful. Most farm equipment had been sold, lost to the banks, or abandoned under dunes of drifting soil. Work was done by horsepower. When disaster struck, even this became scarce. Upon arrival, farmers had unwittingly turned their horses out to feed on the plenitude of uncut grass, not realizing it harboured a disease deadly to the valued animal. Many of them died. Yet another devastating setback in a series of misfortunes.

Struggle for survival was ceaseless, and children worked right alongside their parents. When there was work to do at home, they didn't attend school. Ewen taught students in grades one to eight, but rarely were they all present. On a typical day he had perhaps ten pupils. It was difficult to teach even the basics of the curriculum with attendance so irregular. The conscientious first-year teacher had little choice but to simply give it his best shot. This he did for his entire six months at Partridge Hill, despite the fact that he received not a cent of pay.

Ewen's roommate at Normal School was Roald Ward, also from Wadena. Roald was hired in the school district next to Partridge Hill, just five miles from Ewen. Although the two men had to walk, they visited frequently. It was great not just to have company in the secluded bush, but also to have a colleague with whom to discuss the manifold challenges of teaching.

The two bachelors shared many meals. "Turned out Roald couldn't cook and neither could I," smiles Ewen, "but I did better than he did so he came over to my school most of the time." Ewen's kitchen was outside. There he set up a tripod over an open fire. His cooking pot was a tin can suspended from the tripod by a wire. The sophistication of this equipment matched that of the food that could be prepared using it. Eggs, eggs, and more eggs: always boiled.

Eventually, to both men's relief, the school board came up with a cookstove. Finally Ewen could do some serious cooking. Partridge Hill was aptly named, for it teemed with partridge. With his .22 Ewen had no trouble bagging as many as he pleased. Fortunately, he was good at cooking them too, for partridge was his only source of fresh meat for six months.

Unlike the prolific game bird, water wasn't so accessible. Ewen had to walk to a nearby creek where he and the wildlife shared some very poor quality refreshment.

Chopping wood for heating and cooking was also up to Ewen. The school board supplied a saw and a sawhorse and told him to drag his own trees from the bush.

Ewen and Roald did their shopping on Saturdays. It was tricky buying groceries with no money. The storekeeper in the tiny hamlet nearest Ewen knew the school district was broke, and so wouldn't allow the teachers to buy on credit. There was another store, eleven miles [eighteen km] away, whose proprietor was friendlier. "Jack Stott let us get anything we wanted in the store," Ewen recalls. "We just signed for it and he turned those slips into the municipal office in lieu of taxes, which he said he wasn't paying anyway." Ewen and Roald were forever grateful to Jack for his kindness. If not for him the penniless men couldn't have survived. The Saturday trek to Jack's store, a twenty-two mile (thirty-five km) round trip for Ewen and a little more than half that for Roald, took most of the day. Because they were walking, they selected their groceries carefully. The load going home tended to weigh heavier with the miles.

One day a farmer near Roald's school saw the men setting out on their weekly expedition. Feeling sorry for their plight, he offered them a horse. Neither Ewen nor Roald had ever been on a horse, but they were delighted at the prospect of sparing their feet and legs. When the farmer produced a huge plough horse they were a little taken aback. However, nothing ventured nothing gained. After careful calculation they clambered on its back and proceeded on their way: two men who had never ridden before, on a plough horse with no saddle and no idea of what they were doing. They made it all of one mile (1.6 km) before sheer agony drove them to dismount. The obliging horse continued to amble along with them until, on the return journey, the trio found themselves back at the farmer's gate. Ewen and Roald thanked him sincerely for his favour, but privately decided only to rely on their feet from then on, no matter how far they had to go.

Ewen became good friends with some of the people in the area. He went visiting often. While his own living conditions were barely subsistent, he was appalled by the poverty he saw around him. "Nova" and "Scotia" were two brothers he came to know well. They had come from Nova Scotia with high hopes, only to meet defeat on southern Saskatchewan soil. They lived in a one-room log cabin with Scotia's wife and six children. Their only income was government relief. A mere eight dollars a month to sustain nine people. Despite their penury, Scotia and his family made Ewen welcome in their home. "I went over there for supper a few times," he comments. "Quite often all we had were straight potatoes, not even any butter."

One evening as Ewen approached the school on his way home he noticed all the windows gaping open. A surge of fear enveloped him. Someone had been there. Were they still inside? His thoughts immediately lit on the exconvict. For some time Ewen fretted outside the building, trying to muster the courage to investigate. Not a whisper of sound or movement came from within and finally he cautiously stepped inside. No one was there. Several things, however, were missing, his only suit and his single pair of good shoes among them. He reported the incident to the RCMP, but held little hope of seeing the items again. Eventually the police did recover the shoes. By that time they were in such bad shape that Ewen told the Mounties just to give them back to the thief. In those desperate times, perhaps he needed them more than Ewen anyway.

There was another occasion in which Ewen unwittingly helped his fellow man. Tramping the bush one day with his .22 he came upon five sharp-tailed grouse perched one above the other in a tree. He was astonished. The birds, commonly known as prairie chickens, were usually only seen on the prairie. Ewen remembered once being told that if a prairie chicken was shot with a .22, which gives off little noise, the others around it would look on as it fell but remain calmly on their perches. He decided to try it. Beginning with the lowest, he shot all five birds in succession. Sure enough, the others watched their neighbours fall, but remained motionless on their branches, sensing no danger for themselves. About this time one of the locals came along. His eyes lit up at the sight of Ewen's catch. "Boy, I'd sure like to have one of those!" he exclaimed. "We could sure have a good stew for supper." "How would you like to take the whole five of them?" Ewen replied. "I can get a ruffed grouse anytime. That's what I like better than these sharp-tails." The fellow was delighted. He gathered up all five of the fat birds and went on his way a happy man.

Winter came and snow fell in the bush country. The clean blanket of white made a perfect canvas for the footprints of many wild animals. When Ewen saw all the tracks he had an idea. Perhaps if he tried his hand at trapping he could finally make a little money. A weasel pelt would be worth something, if he could just figure out how to skin it.

Ewen carefully set his trap in the woods. The next day he returned to it, full of anticipation over what he might find. Sure enough, something was there. Close inspection, however, revealed that he had caught a cat. Dismayed but not disheartened, he set the trap again.

This time when he returned he found a small black and white dog, its foot firmly pinned in the trap's jaws. The poor thing was still alive and in great distress. Equally distressed, Ewen made haste to free it. It proved quite a task. The frightened, suffering dog lashed out, snapping and snarling each time Ewen reached to help it. When he finally managed to release the dog he was sick at heart.

Then and there he threw the trap away. Never again would he lay hand to such a cruel instrument.

The beautiful little black and white dog was grateful to his rescuer. While Ewen tried in vain to discover to whom it belonged, the dog already had it figured out. He never left Ewen's side. No one ever claimed him, and soon the two companions were devoted to one another. Ewen named his new friend Teddy. A happy ending to what could have been a tragedy.

Ewen became accustomed to life at Partridge Hill and would have stayed on. However, due to isolation, lack of roads, and harsh winter weather, both his school and Roald's were scheduled to close at Christmas. They wouldn't reopen until April. As the holiday approached, the men made plans to return to Wadena. The immediate question was how? Certainly no bus or train service was available. Even if they had a car it wouldn't do them any good. The few roads around were inaccessible. If they were going to leave then it would have to be by horse. Of course neither of them owned one, and their only experience riding had put them off completely. What to do? Scotia came to the rescue. "He said he would take us back to Wadena cross-country," recalls Ewen. "He didn't have a sleigh but he said he'd build one, and feed his horses, which weren't in good shape, so they'd be ready for the journey."

As it turned out, Scotia was tall on intentions but short on action. He couldn't possibly afford the extra feed, so his horses continued their inadequate diet of slough grass. Not until the night before the trip did he hastily throw together what passed for a sleigh. At 6:00 A.M. the following day Ewen and Roald struggled to cram all their possessions into the uncertain structure. It was barely sufficient for the load. The horses were so gaunt that Ewen doubted they'd survive the forty-five mile (seventy-two km) journey. With some trepidation they set off.

Most of the time there was no road to follow at all. Ewen was amazed that Scotia seemed to know the way intuitively. The trip was grueling. Two tired horses, an overloaded sleigh, three men and a little dog, just dots on the landscape. The deep snow hindered the horses. Once, in frustration and fatigue, they simply sat down.

After hours of exertion the little troupe approached a farm just seven miles (eleven km) from Wadena. The last leg of their journey was before them, but it was getting late, and they needed rest and warmth. Hoping for a little of both they knocked on the farmhouse door.

The man who answered was wary of the sudden appearance of three strangers on his step. He bluntly declared he wouldn't have bums prowling about, and suggested they get off his property. Piqued, Ewen retorted that he and Roald were teachers on their way home after six months of teaching in the north country. If that made them bums then there must be many more such vagrants out there.

At this the farmer was visibly mollified. In a complete about face, he opened his door wide and invited the men inside. His daughters were teachers and any colleague of theirs was more than welcome in his home. In a display of hospitality he treated Ewen, Roald, and Scotia to a fine lunch beside a warm fire. Even the weary horses were escorted to the barn to rest and warm up.

Greatly rejuvenated the travellers continued on their way. The last miles were easy, on a well-travelled road, and the men took the opportunity to stretch their legs by walking. Before they knew it they were at Roald's house. Roald's mother welcomed them with coffee, then Scotia and Ewen carried on to Ewen's home.

Scotia spent a day in each of the two men's homes. His horses, to their great benefit, were sheltered in the town barn, and well fed with oats. When Ewen left Partridge Hill the school board presented him with ten dollars, all they could pull together for his six months' teaching there. Ewen gave the money to Scotia. Ewen's father paid the livery charges for Scotia's team, and gave Scotia an additional ten dollars. Roald and his father also paid Scotia twenty dollars for bringing the men home. After splurging on some shopping in Wadena, Scotia headed back with what amounted to a small fortune in his pocket, the prospect of the best Christmas in years playing joyfully on his mind.

For his part, Ewen was grateful to be home, with comfortable surroundings, ample food on the table, and the company of cherished family and friends. It was with little regret that he ended the incredible adventure of his first teaching experience.

He couldn't tarry long, however, before seeking a new position. After Christmas he set about applying to available schools. It wasn't long before he heard from Pipestone Valley School, near Kelvington, Saskatchewan. Out of 129 applicants, many with far more experience, they had chosen Ewen.

The offer was attractive. Although the school board regretted it could only pay forty dollars a month, the sum came regularly, and Ewen felt rich. "They built a nice little teacherage," he recalls. "It wasn't mine, but it was better than a four-by-eight hole [one by two metre] in the corner of the school." The surroundings were idyllic, and it was a simple matter of a short jaunt into Kelvington to pick up groceries, for which Ewen was always relieved to pay cash.

Ewen often wondered how, at such a young age and with so little experience, he had secured the job at Pipestone Valley over all those other applicants. One day while talking to the chairman of the school board his question was answered. They had narrowed the applications down to two, Ewen's and that of one other fellow who already had eight years' teaching experience. How did they decide who to hire? They flipped a coin.

Social Life

. . . .
. . . .

THE MAJORITY OF teachers who went to teach in country schools left friends and family far behind. They arrived in their new homes to find themselves surrounded by strange faces in a strange land. Stripped of old security systems and support networks, they had to start over, putting down roots and establishing new friendships —no easy task in a rural setting, where houses were few and far between, and householders preoccupied with the numerous demands of a farming lifestyle. In addition, the teacher had the dubious distinction of being regarded as unique; a creature of knowledge from the outside world, whose presence was intriguing yet intimidating. This prevented many close friendships from developing. In fact, in some districts the teacher was never referred to by name. He or she was merely labelled 'The Teacher.' Always under scrutiny, the long-suffering pedagogue worked hard to gain a sense of the social climate of the district and find a place in it.

. . . .

"Teachers were put on a pedestal. If you strayed from the pedestal you'd have people talking about you. It wasn't easy because you'd go there with good intentions, being friendly and so on, and then maybe you were friendly with the wrong people and you'd find the other people against you because of that. But you go in as a stranger. You don't know all these other things that are going on. In those days I think they thought the teachers were somebody special. You were always in the public eye and everyone was watching what you were doing and commenting."

Mary Cooke (nee Sanderson)
Cresco School, Saskatchewan

. . . .

Acceptance of the teacher into the community was crucial to the effective functioning of the school. Those unable to establish a rapport didn't last long. Even the many who did often found life lonely, particularly if used to the bustle of town and city. With the exception of the children during school hours, contact with other human beings was infrequent.

. . . .

"I lived in a teacherage in the school yard beside a community pasture. The only traffic past my little home was cowboys riding to check cattle on the range. They used to hail me when they went by, and occasionally stop and chat if it wasn't school hours."

Laura Filipenko (nee Ganshert)

. . . .

"I was so lonely. Such a gay time I had at Edmonton Normal School. Now the only entertainment [was] a radio with headsets."

Olga Allison (nee Burch)
Wealthy School, Alberta

. . . .

Even teachers who boarded sometimes experienced isolation and loneliness.

. . . .

"My boarding house had two books, the Bible and Hans Brinker and the Silver Skates. *I read every book and text-book in the school."*

Jeana Stanford (nee Russell)
Montpelier School, Alberta

. . . .

"When I returned home at Christmas, I suddenly realized that I hadn't seen a train nor been to town since early July."

Agnes Hunter (nee Burnett)

. . . .

"Since this was an eight-month school I had January and February off. Come March I started back. The first board-ing house was at a family of a young man and wife who

had no children yet. He couldn't speak English but she could speak it quite well. The trouble with this place was that I was in complete isolation. I would come home from school and go right to my bedroom, which was just off the living room, and stay there doing whatever there was for me to do in the way of homework and personal 'desk' business until the Missus. would bring my meal in on a tray and I would eat in solitude in the livingroom. Same thing for breakfast next morning, where I would also be given my lunch for the school. I don't think I saw the Mister more than three times the month that I was required to stay there. As you can assume, I came home from school as late as I could and went to school as early as I could."

Murray Robison
Schlatt School, Alberta

. . . .

The teacher who had a car or access to other transportation, and whose family lived close enough, could travel home weekends.

. . . .

"It was a lonesome life, so I was always anxious to go home on weekends."

Laura Filipenko (nee Ganshert)

. . . .

"I spent many weekends at Chinook with my sister and family and really never suffered from homesickness."

Hazel Youngs (nee Ray)
Longsdale School, Alberta

. . . .

"I was fortunate to be able to get to my home, about twenty miles [thirty-two km], as long as the roads were passable for Dad's Model T."

Camilla Cline (nee Kilborn)
Ribstone Creek School, Alberta

. . . .

"Mr. Symington drove a cutter pulled by one horse. He came every Friday and drove miles delivering the mail. I would drive into Mannville with him quite often, then could go to the Saturday dance. On Sunday my brother drove me back to 'Siberia.'"

Olga Allison (nee Burch)
Wealthy School, Alberta

. . . .

Degree of social life varied by district. Some continually sought opportunities to gather, while others were less eager to socialize as a community or even individuals. Teachers had no choice but to conform to each rural temperament. As they often remained at a school only one to three years, over the course of time they experienced several social environments.

. . . .

*"The two things I remember are the lack of anything to
read and no social life at all. My next place was a delight-
ful place to be as the people were very helpful and sociable. There were books I could borrow from a retired sea
captain and young people to make friends with."*

Ruth Cowan (nee Hawkins)

. . . .

*"Social life was very good at Benton and we had United
Church services and I had a CGIT group. Dolemead wasn't
much for social life. The farms were bigger and people
tended to go to Calgary for their activities."*

Ruth Keiver (nee Coffin)

. . . .

Some districts had a hall, but in many cases the schoolhouse was the only public building in the area, and the
natural locale for community events. This was awkward for
teachers who lived on the premises. Not only did they
have no choice about attending the affair, but their home
was considered public domain, needed for making coffee,
preparing lunch, and putting small sleepy-heads to bed
until their parents were ready to leave, sometimes not
until dawn. Eileen Toliver (then Barkley) tells of returning
to "a well-watered bed" on such occasions.

The school was used for political meetings, church
services, box socials, picnics, and card parties. Occasionally

entertainment was billed as a fundraiser, in which case usually only the men paid a small admission fee.

A favourite in many districts was the Friday night dance. The floor was sprinkled with cornmeal or wax shavings to make it suitable for dancing and people brought gas lanterns for light. Leaving their hardships behind, they danced the night away.

. . . .

"It was a wonderful district, all families on the same level struggling to survive. I had such a good boarding house and there were many community events, many house parties and card parties and dances in the school. To attend a function at the school cost the men twenty-five cents and the ladies provided lunch. There were many young people and a good community spirit."

Camilla Cline (nee Kilborn)
Rough Meadow School, Alberta

. . . .

"In order to raise money for the bags of candy given as a treat by Santa at the end of the Christmas Concert, card parties were held at the school. Desks were put together to form tables, players brought their own cards, prizes were a turkey or a home-cured ham. Sometimes a quilt made by the ladies would be raffled. Whist was the popular game. Each man paid twenty-five cents, the ladies brought sandwiches and cakes. Coffee bought at twenty-five cents a pound, or exchanged for a bushel

*of wheat, was made in a wash boiler, simmering away on
the stove all evening. Whole families came. Babies were
put to sleep on coats at the back. Small children played
until they too slept. Everyone enjoyed the late lunch
before hitching up the teams to wagons or sleighs for the
ride home."*

Hazel McKenzie (nee Watson)
Ridgeway School, Alberta

. . . .

*"In the fall it was traditional to have a Thanksgiving
supper and two professors came from the university for
the weekend. After an evening dinner one entertained
by reciting favourite poems. Then on Sunday the other
one baptized all the new babies."*

Ruth Cowan (nee Hawkins)

. . . .

*"Dances were held in the school every Friday night. I
went home every weekend to help my mother who was
expecting a baby. A boy was born December 6th, so
from then on I attended the dances. They danced a lot
of square dances. The first dance I went to they put
me in a square where the girls were swung and twirled.
The plan was to get the teacher dizzy. However, it
didn't work."*

Jeana Stanford (nee Russell)
Montpelier School, Alberta

. . . .

"Dances were often held at the school on Friday nights, so the children's desks were piled up at the side of the room. On Monday mornings everything was confusion, sorting out everyone's belongings."

Dorothy Howarth (nee Gaetz)

. . . .

"Everyone enjoyed the parties and dances at the school on Friday nights. Volunteers supplied the music and the ladies brought lunch."

Muriel Lugg (nee Smith)
Chailey School, Alberta

. . . .

"All social events were held in the hall. It was a very small, unpainted building with a shed attached to serve as a kitchen and an annex on the side with a bench around its three sides. Everyone and his children would come to the community dances held about every month. The babies would be put to sleep on the benches, which were also used for piling outer garments during the cold weather. How some of those babies survived under the coats I'll never know. Some of the women would be busy out in the kitchen preparing the lunch, which was always served at midnight. Meanwhile some of the men would be going out to the cars and wagons to swill a little home brew. These dances would go on until the wee hours of the morning."

Murray Robison
Abelein School, Alberta

. . . .

In a socially lively district the teacher's participation was always in demand. Many brought unique talent to their areas, and many more joined in just for the fun of it.

. . . .

"I boarded at Ridley's, three quarters of a mile [one km] from school. I was almost a monotone. Hence I would try to sing as I walked all the way to school and back again. I succeeded so well that when the ladies had a party I was asked to sing a solo. I gracefully declined and said I would recite for them. They asked for more. I had taken elocution lessons so was happy to recite several selections."

Jeana Stanford (nee Russell)
Montpelier School, Alberta

. . . .

"During the long winter months once a week some older children came to my teacherage to play crokinole. They enjoyed the game and tried to excel their skill."

Annie Tym (nee Sankey)
Jewett School, Alberta

. . . .

"Often on Sunday afternoons we would have softball tournaments, the neighbours joining in too."

Laura Filipenko (nee Ganshert)

. . . .

*"The surrounding districts were very friendly so that
schoolhouse dances, box socials, Christmas concerts were
always well attended. In my district we usually produced
a play during winter months. Entrance fee twenty-five
cents."*

Mabel Spady (nee Hemeyer)
Park Springs School, Alberta

. . . .

*"The Anglican Young People had a very active group in
this district. They held dances; every year put on a three
act play and I took part in it."*

Ruth Keiver (nee Coffin)
New Valley School, Alberta

. . . .

*"The district put on plays. I was the heroine in one. All
the love scenes were cut out because the hero was in love
with the director's daughter."*

Jeana Stanford (nee Russell)
Sherburne School, Alberta

. . . .

*"There was very little in the so-called town of Pashley—
the elevator agent who also ran the post office and a
family by the name of Reid. On Sundays it was just
assumed that all the young bucks and gals would gather
at the Reid home and have a good social time. There
would always be plenty of fun and games and Mrs. Reid
always had some kind of goodies to serve up."*

Murray Robison
Abelein School, Alberta

. . . .

Because many regions were settled by people of diverse
ethnic origin, the teacher sometimes enjoyed the opportunity to sample different cultural traditions.

. . . .

*"For me, the highlight of the week was Saturday night
when, instead of a bath in a wash tub by the kitchen
stove, a neighbour would invite us to come for a sauna
bath. There were a number of Finns in our district who
had brought their custom of sauna bathing with them
from Finland. Soon several families had built small
wooden saunas of two rooms, the outer one for dressing,
the larger one with a stove and tiers of benches ascending
almost to the ceiling. A tub of cold water with a dipper to
spatter it on the red-hot stove provided clouds of steam.
As the heat and steam increased, the more hardy souls
moved up gradually to the higher benches, while some of
us were content to go no more than half way. We washed
thoroughly before steaming, and again after, our bodies*

shiny red and oozing with perspiration. A dipper full of cold water was thrown over us before going to the other room to dress. Men and women went in separately, in two groups. After the steaming, the men usually ran out-side before dressing to roll in the snow to prevent colds. Then we crowded into the farmhouse kitchen to play cards, dance, visit and have coffee. With shiny faces and stringy wet hair we had a lovely time!"

Hazel McKenzie (nee Watson)
Ridgeway School, Alberta

. . . .

Whether boarding or living alone, the teacher was often invited to students' homes for a meal or even a weekend. Sometimes it was only district protocol that "The Teacher" be invited over at least once. More often, however, it was due to sincere hospitality. This did much to ease any loneliness.

. . . .

"Social life in the area was good. There were dances, card games, ball games, and I was included everywhere."

Hazel Youngs (nee Ray)
Longsdale School, Alberta

. . . .

*"Every spring this district had a school picnic as well as a
Sports League Day. People were sociable and cooperated
in every way. I was invited out to many suppers. During
the long cold winters I spent many weekends visiting
children's homes. We became real friends."*

Annie Tym (nee Sankey)
Jewett School, Alberta

. . . .

In time most teachers became comfortably assimilated
into the social life of their district; some even married
and settled down locally. Those who were less content
were relieved to move on sooner rather than later, and
inevitably found happier circumstances elsewhere.

Linnea's Story

. . . .
. . . .

LINNEA HAGGLUND'S FAMILY was better off than many during the Great Depression. In 1932 they opened the Waterton Bungalow Camp in Waterton Lakes National Park, Alberta. Linnea and her siblings worked hard alongside their parents to make the camp viable. Nevertheless, when they all left home in 1935, Linnea to Calgary Normal School, her sister to grade twelve in Bellevue and her brother to school in Vancouver, Mr. Hagglund cashed in a life insurance policy to keep his children in room and board. Even with a successful business, times were tight.

In the summer of 1936, Linnea returned to Waterton and puzzled over how she might find work in her chosen profession. She knew it would be difficult, but she had one advantage. Mr. Bremner, the school inspector for southern Alberta, vacationed at the bungalow camp each year. He was happy to give her a list of all the schools hiring new teachers in his inspectorate.

Willing to go the extra mile, and taking Waterton school teacher Rose Blair with her, Linnea travelled to every school on the list, stopping at the home of each board chairman to make her application personally. It was a long, tiring day. Many times they waited while the chairman finished his farm work, then took time to wash up before meeting them. All listened to what Linnea had to say; none offered her a position. It was well past midnight before the weary travellers returned home.

The following day Mr. Bremner asked about the trip, and when Linnea had nothing positive to report he made a proposal. "He asked if I would be willing to teach grades one to eleven for six hundred dollars a year," says Linnea. "I told him I would gladly teach for my board to get some experience." In a twinkling the contract was signed and Linnea became the new schoolmistress of Schaffer School, ten miles (sixteen km) west of Claresholm. She was walking on air!

Then the Woodhouse School, south of Claresholm, approached her with a much more attractive offer: $750 for teaching just nine grades. Linnea's levity vanished. Having already committed herself to Schaffer, she reluctantly turned Woodhouse down.

Her disappointment was keen, but as she thought about Schaffer it gradually gave way to excited anticipation. She was to board at Kerr's, home of the school board chairman. "Mr. Kerr told me that if I did the janitor work at the school I would get another five dollars a month," she recalls. "So I arrived a few days early to clean the school and check the 'library.'"

The school was a mile and a half (2.5 km) from Kerr's. A stone's throw from it lived the Hilgers, whose boys received five dollars a month to start the fire and bring a bucket of water daily. On the first day of school the board told Linnea they couldn't pay ten dollars a month for janitor, fire, and water duties. Somebody would have to do it all for just five dollars. The Hilger boys were the obvious choice; they had to bring the water anyway. So as quickly as she took them on, Linnea was relieved of her custodial chores.

She had twelve students. Three of the boys and one girl were almost the same age as she. They should have been in grade eleven, but having failed several grade ten subjects the year before, they were taking courses in both grades.

To complicate matters, the boys didn't show up until six weeks after school began because they had jobs on a threshing crew and didn't want to give up the income. When they finally did arrive they took pains to demonstrate their unwillingness to be there. They refused to recite the Lord's Prayer each morning. Linnea knew their families were all religious, but the boys fell back on the School Act, claiming it said religion couldn't be forced upon students. They were disrespectful, sniggeringly referring to her as "Schoolmarm" behind her back. They tried everything to get themselves expelled, but Linnea knew she could never oblige them. Each boy's father was on the school board, and expelling them would surely result in her own expulsion. She was fighting a losing battle, made worse by trying to bring the uncooperative boys up to speed on six weeks of lost work.

To add to her troubles many other students had problems as well. One grade five boy had never finished a book, and two children had severe learning disabilities. Sparse materials didn't help. "The library could be listed as nonexistent," Linnea states. "There were a few old books on a shelf, probably donated by someone, but nothing that could be considered a reference book." With so much working against her she quickly became discouraged. "I would gladly have quit and gone home, but I knew if I gave up this job my teaching career was over. I would never get another chance!"

Thoroughly miserable, she persevered, and wracked her brains for solutions to her problems. One presented itself quickly. If she gave up her noon break and recesses, she could maximize instructional time. She sent the little ones out for recess early and continued to teach the high school students. When the lower grades returned she sent the older students out. Doing the same thing at noon, she made the most of every teaching minute. Although it meant rushing through her own lunch, the system worked well, and the trade off in improved learning was worth it.

Things would have begun looking up, but a dark shadow loomed on the horizon. Halloween. A traditional time for pranks, it was the perfect chance for the recalcitrant high school boys to thwart Linnea and she was certain they would try. She made up her mind to ignore their tricks—no matter what—and braced herself for the worst. Bright and early Halloween morning the fun began. "The boys had gotten some very fine wire—almost invisible," Linnea recalls. "This they strung across the aisles almost everywhere. When I went from one class to another, and down the aisle, I ran into this invisible wire. Usually it broke. I never let on I'd noticed it." Sticking to her resolve, Linnea continued to walk the aisles, teaching in her usual manner, not a trace of disturbance on her face.

The boys were stymied but not defeated. Their arsenal also included fire crackers. The wire was forgotten as sudden, sporadic blasts shattered the working silence. The students inevitably reacted, but Linnea's expression didn't flicker. She calmly carried on. In desperation the "janitor" tossed a whole string of fire crackers into the blazing stove. A volley of explosions tore the air. Linnea remained unmoved.

This was too much for the boys. They began breaking the crackers in half, lighting them in the middle, and sending them spluttering across the floor in every direction. When Linnea still didn't respond Edgar Hilger aimed one of the doctored crackers directly at her feet. "It skittered down the aisle," Linnea says, "coming to a stop when it hit my shoe. Sparks flashed up my legs but I refused to move. Silk stockings were one dollar a pair and on my wages that was quite a sum. The boys could see runs all up and down my stockings—wherever a spark had landed. I made no mention of it."

A sudden silence descended over the classroom. Not only were the boys having no fun, due to Linnea's lack of attention, but with the ruined stockings they knew they had gone too far. After school Edgar shamefacedly apologized, offering to replace the tattered hose. Politely and with dignity Linnea turned him down. From that point on her problems with the boys were over. In fact, they made a complete about face and became eager to help her in every way possible. She had won!

But the big boys weren't the only problem Linnea faced. One day she caught a grade five student misbehaving at her desk. She instinctively reached out and gave the girl a smart smack on the head. Stunned and aggrieved, the girl made sure Linnea heard her that recess bitterly proclaim to her friends that the School Act forbade punishment on anything but the hands. Her father, also a trustee, was going to hear about this! Linnea, however, was one step ahead. "When we resumed classes," she says, "I told her that if she wished I would apologize to her for slapping her on the head and strap her instead." The mortified girl declined the invitation, and never again caused trouble in the classroom.

Linnea now enjoyed the utmost respect of all her pupils. They cooperated in every way and became a pleasure to teach. She knew that a rural teacher was regarded as a role model in the community, and was careful to conduct herself appropriately. She neither drank nor smoked. But she was astounded to discover the true extent of her influence. Accustomed to parting her hair down the side, she decided one day to try a middle part. Within a week every single student was wearing his or her hair parted exactly the same way!

Linnea's students loved to hunt gophers, hawks, and crows for the government bounty. One of the less pleasant aspects of her job was counting and recording these captures. The tails were bound together in bunches of ten, the birds' feet in pairs, and tiny egg cartons were provided for the broken shells. Linnea carefully counted each of these, entered the tallies on government forms and signed them. At the first opportunity the children presented their forms in Claresholm to claim their money. Though never a large amount, for some it was cherished pocket money, while for others, much needed additional family income.

Gopher snaring was new to Linnea. At first she didn't know what the students were doing when she encountered them scattered flat on their stomachs throughout the schoolyard. She soon learned. "Each was watching a snare set at the mouth of a gopher hole," she explains. "One boy was pouring water down another hole. Finally a gopher came up and was caught in one of the snares. Another recess, the children came dashing in all excited. The gopher that had come out of the hole was a mother, who delivered her young while they pulled the snare. They wondered if they could collect for the young too." Such were the realities of rural life in the thirties.

The challenges Linnea faced at school were balanced by a happy home life. The Kerrs had boarded the teacher for years and were comfortable with her presence. They drew her into their daily activities like one of the family. Linnea accommodated herself to their lifestyle with ease. Saturday was the best day of the week. "All the farmers and their families converged on Claresholm every Saturday night," she fondly recalls. "Everyone visited everyone else; you knew without a doubt that all your friends and neighbours would be there. One could sit in the car on the street and watch the world go by. Young couples walked up and down, arm in arm."

There was no money to shop, or even buy a cup of coffee, but it was a chance for children to gaze at the wonders in store windows, sweethearts to meet, and friends and relatives to reunite. Mrs. Kerr especially enjoyed the chance to visit family members living east of Claresholm where she had grown up. Even Linnea's students stopped to say hello. "Now out of class the 'Schoolmarm' was said to my face with a tone of respect," she laughs, "almost like it was an honoured title they had bestowed on me."

Sunday was a day of rest. Breakfast and morning chores complete, the entire family assembled before the radio in the living room to listen to "Back to the Bible," broadcast by Premier William Aberhart. This was church, a scenario repeated in many rural homes throughout the province. They followed the scriptures in their bibles, sang all the hymns, and devoutly uttered "Amen" after bowing their heads for each prayer. The afternoon broadcast was solemnized the same way. In lieu of a weekly collection, the family mailed a donation to the Bible Institute in Calgary once a month. The day progressed quietly. Lunch and supper were simple meals, prepared the day before. Evening chores were completed, and gently and reverently, Sunday came to a tranquil close.

Winter arrived and with it deep snows. Linnea continued to walk to school. Inspector Bremner considered it improper for a lady to teach in slacks, but Linnea couldn't make the long trek otherwise without getting soaked and risking chilblains. Leaving a skirt at the school, she wore ski pants for her walk there, then changed in the girls' outhouse. Many of the female students who rode horseback did the same.

Time came for the annual Christmas concert and Linnea wanted to make sure her first efforts went smoothly. Turning to the Kerrs for advice, she learned that the board provided oranges and candy for the children and the school owned a Santa suit. The teacher, however, was expected to purchase a gift for each child out of her own money.

From a salary of sixty dollars a month Linnea paid twenty dollars room and board and set aside that and more for required summer school courses the following year. Then there were her on-going personal expenses to consider, as well as the cost of getting home for Christmas and that of her own Christmas shopping.

Linnea carefully reviewed her budget. After much deliberation she decided she could spend ten dollars on the children of the district, seventy-five cents for each of twelve students and one child not yet in school. She made her purchases through the Eaton's catalogue.

The day of the concert arrived. Excitement laced the air, and butterflies danced in the stomachs of all the young performers and their teacher. Linnea needn't have worried. Before such an appreciative audience all couldn't help but go well. Just when she thought her satisfaction complete, Edgar Hilger stood before the crowd. He and the other high school boys had a special announcement.

"I was very surprised when he called me up front and presented me with a pointer," Linnea remembers. "It was wrapped in brown paper. He told how the boys had made it from a hardwood rod from inside a roll of oilcloth. It was as smooth as one purchased from a supply store." Linnea was overwhelmed. At that moment she knew she had truly won their hearts. The pointer became one of her most cherished possessions.

In the audience that night were Linnea's sister, Esther, her high school sweetheart, Frank Goble, and a friend, George Annand. They were attending school in Calgary and on their way home for the holidays. After the concert Linnea joined them and they headed home together in George's old car. Linnea's spirits were light. Her first four months teaching were behind her and the road ahead looked bright.

It stormed continuously throughout the holiday. When it came time to leave for school again Linnea, Esther, Frank and George decided to set out a day early due to the poor conditions. "It took us all day to get to Pincher Creek, a distance of thirty-five miles [fifty-six km]," she recalls. "The boys shovelled and we pushed a good part of the way. It seemed the road was one long snowdrift. When we got to

Pincher Creek we knew it was too late to go any farther." Linnea phoned the Kerrs to say she wouldn't make it that night. Mr. Kerr told her cars couldn't get through from Claresholm to the Schaffer district anyway. He'd meet her the following day in Claresholm with horse and sleigh. Sunday morning dawned with a high wind. The four waited for the grader to pass, then fell in behind it along with a string of other cars. "The wind was drifting the snow so badly," Linnea states, "the last cars had trouble getting through. It was late afternoon before we got to Claresholm, a distance of sixty or seventy miles."

Once again Linnea phoned the Kerrs. It was too late for Mr. Kerr to come and get her. The twenty-mile (thirty-two km) round trip would take several hours. He told Linnea to spend the night in Claresholm and he'd pick her up in the morning.

Being rural, the Kerrs were on a telephone party line. It was common in those days for neighbours to pick up and listen to one another's calls. Suddenly Mr. Fenton's voice crackled over the line. The snow was too deep even for horses, he said. He would pick Linnea up himself with his more sure-footed team of mules. Thus Linnea finally made it back to her school, albeit a day late. The children were grateful for the extra holiday but soon learned they'd have to make it up at Easter. The much depended upon government grant would be lost if the school didn't operate its full two hundred days.

The second half of Linnea's year went smoothly. She became more and more confident as a teacher. Proof of her success came in June when all of her formerly failing high school students passed their departmental exams in Claresholm.

Linnea's reputation was growing, and by the end of the term she was invited to teach at the Grain Belt School, east of Claresholm, the following year: nine grades for $840. She was delighted. The chairman of the Grain Belt school board, Mr. Chilton, was Mrs. Kerr's brother. Linnea happily accepted the Chiltons' offer to board her. She already knew them from Saturday nights in Claresholm with the Kerrs.

Before she could move to Grain Belt Linnea had summer school in Edmonton. Teachers were expected to attend in order to acquire skills for instructing new courses in the curriculum: music, drama, typing and bookkeeping. Linnea had been saving for months to cover the course and dormitory costs. Now she learned she'd have to purchase her own equipment as well. Typing was done to music. She picked up some records, and managed to find a phonograph and typewriter, both secondhand, for thirty-five dollars. The expense of summer school was taxing, but the anticipation of her handsome pay raise eased the strain.

When the new term began, Linnea found Grain Belt very agreeable. The children were respectful and had no educational difficulties. Linnea still walked a mile and a half (2.5 km) to school but, like the Kerrs, the Chiltons embraced her as one of their own. They lived in a large house equipped with electric lights and indoor plumbing. With these added conveniences, Linnea didn't mind paying an extra five dollars a month room and board.

She continued to enjoy Saturday evenings in Claresholm, this time accompanying the Chiltons. She often left, however, with the Kerrs, who missed their friend and former lodger. Many times she spent Saturday night with them and they returned her to the Chiltons Sunday evening.

Others from Schaffer missed Linnea too. One day Edgar Hilger invited her to a card party at the school. He was the proud new owner of a used jalopy and offered to pick her up in Grain Belt and take her home again. It was on a Wednesday, and Linnea hesitated about going out midweek, but she didn't want to disappoint Edgar.

The card party was fun. Linnea's former students were delighted to see her. They lavished her with attention. Once again she witnessed the influence a teacher has as they hung on her every word. The subject of smoking came up. Linnea declared that she did not and would not smoke. Years later one of those former students confided in her that not one of them ever started smoking.

The joke was on Linnea that evening. She triumphed at whist and won the grand prize: a glass ashtray. She laughingly donated it back to the school board for use at another card party. It was past midnight before Edgar got her home. Mrs. Chilton was quick to deliver words of reproof. Linnea was temporarily chastised, but it had been a lovely evening.

One day Linnea was surprised to receive a letter from the Alberta Teachers Association (ATA). Why, they inquired, had she signed a contract with the Schaffer School for six hundred dollars when they were authorized to pay eight hundred dollars? Linnea declared her ignorance of the matter, but the ATA wouldn't let it go. They said they would withhold the Schaffer grant until the two hundred dollars owing Linnea was paid. The Schaffer board was sincere in its claim that the district was too poor to come up with the money. Months of negotiations between the two governing bodies ensued. Finally a compromise was reached and Linnea was issued a cheque for $158.

The thrill of the sudden windfall was tempered by her knowledge that the Schaffer district now truly suffered. The teacher replacing her was forced to board in the homes of residents whose taxes were overdue. When this brought them up to owing only three years' back taxes, she moved on to the next destitute home. "None of the homes had a spare bedroom," Linnea points out, "so she found herself sleeping with two or three of the students she was teaching." It was a sad situation, but one over which Linnea had no control.

Christmas approached and she again thought about the annual concert. Her plans for staging it were thwarted, however, when one by one her students mysteriously fell ill. After a few days' absence they returned to school apparently healthy, but exhibiting a strange symptom: skin peeling between their fingers. The health nurse was called to investigate. She declared a mild outbreak of scarlet fever and promptly closed the school. Students and teacher had to go to Claresholm for a shot. The school wasn't reopened until January. No Christmas Concert that year!

The following year Linnea made up for the disappointment. The animations of a man named Walt Disney were becoming increasingly popular. A recent release featured a lazy grasshopper neglecting to prepare for winter. Linnea used that theme to script a play, creating characters to match the number and age of her students. She obtained sheet music for "The World Owes Me a Living," a song the grasshopper frequently rendered on his violin, and gave it to Billy Chilton, a young violin student, requesting that it become his lesson until the time of the concert.

With a squirrel, bumblebee, and various other creatures making up the cast, costumes were a special challenge. Every conceivable material was used. Linnea even resorted to modifying her old dresses.

On the night of the concert the grasshopper, complete with clothes hanger antennae, gave a stellar performance. Ill prepared for winter, he caught a terrible cold and his concerned companions set out to nurse him back to health. A washtub stood on the stage; a kettle of water, at full boil, sat on the wood burning stove. The young actors seized the kettle and poured boiling water into the tub. Then they thrust the grasshopper's feet into it. He immediately let forth a blood-curdling shriek and yanked his feet from the tub. The audience was horrified. Surely the young boy had been burned! How could the teacher allow such a thing? Then the grasshopper screwed up his face, opened his mouth wide, and sneezed. As his disengaged antenna went sailing out over the crowd, the audience realized he was only acting. But what about the boiling water? It wasn't until after the performance the mystery was solved. A wooden block, unseen by the audience, had been placed in the tub to keep the grasshopper's feet elevated above the water. It was a Christmas concert the whole district remembered for years to come.

That year, Linnea and Frank Goble were married. In order to free more jobs for men during the depression, married women, unless they could prove they were the main breadwinners of the family, weren't allowed to teach. Some who were desperate for income got around this by living away from their husbands and families under the pretext of being single. Linnea, however, didn't have to resort to such measures.

Any regret she felt at having to abandon her career was more than matched by that of the residents of the Grain

Belt district. Their appreciation of her was expressed in a huge shower thrown by Mrs. Chilton. Every person in the district came bearing gifts and bidding fond farewells. It was an appropriate conclusion to three years of teaching success.

For Linnea, 1939 represented both an ending and a beginning. It was the same for all rural teachers of Alberta and Saskatchewan. After ten long years the drought and depression were finally drawing to a close. At the same time, the onset of World War II was launching yet another unique era in the history of country schools and those who taught in them.

. . . .

DATE DUE
DATE DE RETOUR

AUG - 1 2001	
SEP - 5 2001	
SEP 2 5 2001	
DEC 3 2001	
JUN 2 1 2003	

Printed and bound
in Boucherville, Quebec, Canada by
MARC VEILLEUX IMPRIMEUR INC.
in September, 1999